First Edition

THE FIRST SURGEONS: THE EVOLUTION OF OPERATIVE SKILL AND INSTRUMENTATION IN EARLY MEDICINE

Dr. Umer Hamid Wani MS *(General Surgery)*

Assistant Professor

Department of Ilmul Jarahat (Surgery)

Institute of Asian Medical Sciences (IAMS)

Srinagar, J & K, India

Email: hatimjas66@gmail.com

Dr. Saiyad Shah Alam MS *(General Surgery)*

Director

National Institute of Unani Medicine (NIUM)

Bangalore, Karnataka, India

Dr. Firdous Ahmad Najar MS *(General Surgery)*

Associate Professor & HoD

Department of Ilmul Jarahat (Surgery)

National Institute of Unani Medicine (NIUM)

Bangalore, Karnataka, India

They said, "Exalted are You; we have no knowledge except what You have taught us. Indeed, it is You (Allah) who is the Knowing, the Wise."
Surah Al-Baqarah Ayat 32
(Al Quran)

"Dedicated to the voices that guided, the hands that steadied, and the hearts that inspired—my life's tapestry is woven with your threads."

Preface

Surgery is the most eloquent dialogue between intellect and touch. Across epochs and empires, a practiced hand and a curious mind have met at the wound's edge to probe, to mend, and—above all—to understand. *The First Surgeons: The Evolution of Operative Skill and Instrumentation in Early Medicine* is my attempt to trace that dialogue from its first whispered questions to the confident cadence of medieval operating rooms.

Why this book—and why now? Because the modern scalpel, dazzling in its precision, too easily hides its ancestry. Buried beneath steel and silicon lie reeds from the Nile, bronze knives from the Ganges, tempered irons from Córdoba, and diamond-tipped lithotrites from Mughal ateliers. Each carries a story of observation, experiment, and hard-won humility. To forget those stories is to narrow our professional imagination.

This work pursues three guiding aims:

1. **Restore context.** Surgical history did not advance along a single Western line; it was braided from

Egyptian pragmatism, Indian craftsmanship, Greco-Arab science, and Indo-Persian synthesis.

2. **Let artefacts testify.** Instruments are treated as primary texts—decoded for ergonomics, material science, and the clinical philosophy they embody.

3. **Translate relevance.** Wherever possible, ancient procedures are mapped to modern principles: triage, asepsis, anesthesia, hemostasis, and postoperative care.

The structure reflects that mission.

- **Chapter 1** dissects the rational trauma (Surgery) manual of the 3,600-year-old *Edwin Smith Papyrus*.
- **Chapter 2** revisits Sushruta's surgical school, highlighting techniques that pre-empted plastic and vascular surgery.
- **Chapter 3** profiles six giants of the Islamic Golden Age—from al-Razi's clinical audacity to Ibn al-Quff's inhalational anesthesia—illustrating nearly 200 instruments in the process.
- **Chapter 4** follows the transmission and transformation of these ideas in India, culminating

in the richly illustrated Mughal treatise *Tibb-e-Dara-Shikohi*.

Gratitude, like history, is layered—each thread woven with memory, meaning, and quiet resilience. This work began as a pursuit of knowledge, but it became something far more intimate: a journey through forgotten corridors of healing, guided by the steady hands and sharp minds of those who believed in its worth.

I am indebted to **Director & Professor Saiyad Shah Alam** and **Dr. Firdous Ah Najar**, my co-authors and collaborators, for opening doors to long-neglected pages and for their unwavering intellectual companionship. Their insight and encouragement shaped this book from its earliest whispers into its final voice.

To my colleagues and residents, who kept the inquiry grounded in honesty and discipline—thank you for being its conscience. And to my students, whose curiosity lit up even the most obscure questions—you gave the work its pulse and promise.

Most deeply, I thank my family. In moments of solitude, when the weight of time and task threatened to overwhelm, it was your quiet faith that turned isolation into clarity and urgency into purpose. You made this possible in ways words can only attempt to honor.

May the chapters that follow serve not merely as a chronicle of knowledge but as an invitation—to pick up the thread of inquiry, to revere the legacy of First surgeons, and to shape the instruments of tomorrow with the same courage, compassion, and discernment our forebears once wielded.

> Let the Surgeon be bold in all sure things, & fearful in dangerous things, let him avoid all faulty treatments & practices. He ought to be gracious to the sick, considerate to his associates, cautions in his prognostications. Let him be modest. Dignified, gentle, pitiful, merciful; neither covetous nor an extortionist of money; but rather let his reward be according to his work, to the means of the patient, to the quality of the issue, & to his own dignity.
>
> -Ars Chirurgica

Umer Hamid Wani

Contents

Where Surgery Began: The Scientific Approach of the Edwin Smith Papyrus (3,600 year old)

The Edwin Smith Papyrus (***Bardi noshta***), is the oldest known medical and surgical treatise, dating to around 1600 BCE, during Dynasties 16–17 of the Second Intermediate Period in ancient Egypt.[1] Unlike other ancient medical texts, which often blended magic and medicine, the Edwin Smith Papyrus is notable for its rational, scientific approach to trauma and surgery.[2] It is named after Edwin Smith, an American Egyptologist who purchased the document in Luxor, Egypt, in 1862 from a local dealer.[1] The papyrus is now housed at the New York Academy of Medicine and is considered a critical piece of medical history, shedding light on ancient Egyptian medical practices and surgical techniques.[3]

Edwin Smith Papyrus

Plates vi & vii of the Edwin Smith Papyrus at the Rare Book Room, New York Academy of Medicine[3]. Size: length: 4.68 meters, Created c. 1600 BC. Discovered Egypt, Present location New York City, New York, United States.

The papyrus, measuring approximately 4.68 meters (15.3 feet) in length, is written in hieratic script, a cursive form of Egyptian hieroglyphs. It was originally folded into a scroll with 17 columns of 377 lines on the recto (front) side and 5 columns of 92 lines on the verso (back) side. The text primarily deals with trauma, presenting 48 clinical cases

involving injuries to the head, neck, arms, torso, and spine.
[4]

Authorship and Historical Context:

The authorship of the papyrus remains debated, but it is believed to be a copy of a much older text, possibly dating back to the Old Kingdom (c. 3000–2500 BCE). Some scholars, including James Henry Breasted, who first translated the papyrus in 1930, have speculated that the original author could have been Imhotep, the famous architect, physician, and polymath of the Old Kingdom, although this remains unproven. The language and terminology used in the papyrus suggest it was copied from an earlier manuscript, evidenced by archaic grammar and medical terms. [4]

List of cases

As listed in [5, 8]

- Head (27 cases, the first incomplete)
- Skull, overlying soft tissue and brain, Cases 1-10.
- Nose, Cases 11-14.

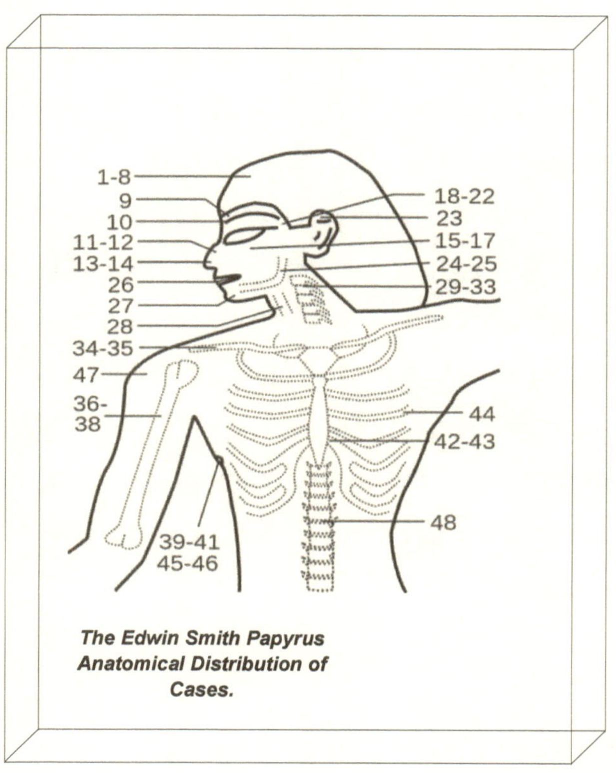

**The Edwin Smith Papyrus
Anatomical Distribution of
Cases.**

- Maxillary region, Cases 15-17
- Temporal region, Cases 18-22.
- Ears, mandible, lips and chin, Cases 23-27.
- Throat and Neck (Cervical Vertebrae), Cases 28-33.
- Clavicle, Cases 34-35.
- Humerus, Cases 36-38.

- Sternum, Overlying Soft Tissue, & True Ribs, Cases 39-46.
- Shoulders, Case 47.
- Spinal Column, Case 48 (incomplete).

The papyrus describes the types of injuries, their examination, diagnosis, prognosis, and treatment. In addition, the verso side includes magical spells and medical prescriptions, though these make up a minor portion of the text compared to its surgical content.

Content and Structure:

The 48 cases detailed in the Edwin Smith Papyrus are organized in descending anatomical order, starting with injuries to the head and moving down to the spine. Each case is methodically described with the following components:

1. **Title:** Describes the type of injury (e.g., "Practices for a gaping wound in his head, which has penetrated to the bone and split the skull").

2. **Examination:** The physician examines the injury using visual, olfactory, and tactile methods, such as palpation and pulse-taking.

3. Diagnosis: The physician makes a diagnosis based on the examination and determines whether the injury is treatable. There are three categories of prognosis:

- *"An ailment which I will treat."*
  - *"An ailment with which I will contend."*
  - *"An ailment not to be treated."*

4. Treatment: Provides detailed instructions on how to treat the injury. This often includes suturing wounds, bandaging, applying splints, using poultices, and stopping bleeding with raw meat, and applying honey to prevent infection.

5. Glossary: Clarifies any obscure medical terms used in the description.

The cases also include explanations of the injuries and their potential causes, offering insight into the Egyptians' advanced understanding of trauma. For example, the papyrus discusses the effects of head injuries on motor functions, with some of the earliest references to the brain, its coverings (*jumjuma*=meninges), cerebrospinal fluid, and intracranial pulsations. The text also recognizes the relationship between injuries to specific parts of the brain and paralysis on the opposite side of the body—a significant observation in the history of neurology.

Surgical Techniques and Treatments: [4]

The papyrus provides detailed descriptions of various surgical techniques, demonstrating the Egyptians' deep knowledge of anatomy and medical practice. Among the treatments described are:

- Suturing: Used for injuries to the lips, throat, and shoulder.
- Splints: Applied to fractures to immobilize bones, particularly in the head, spine, and limbs.
- Poultices and Bandages: Applied to wounds to promote healing and prevent infection.
- Raw Meat: Used to stop bleeding, especially in deep wounds.
- Honey: Applied to wounds as an antimicrobial to prevent infection.

The text's emphasis on rational medical treatment, based on observation and examination, marks a significant departure from the magical treatments found in other contemporary medical texts, such as the Ebers Papyrus. However, magic is not entirely absent from the Edwin Smith Papyrus; it appears in the form of spells and incantations on the verso side and in a few cases of particularly severe or untreatable conditions.

Advanced Medical Knowledge:

One of the most remarkable aspects of the Edwin Smith Papyrus is its detailed anatomical and physiological observations. The document contains the first known references to the brain, describing its structure and function. It also discusses the role of the heart and its relationship to the pulse (*nabz*), highlighting the Egyptians' understanding of circulation. The papyrus also recognizes the link between spinal injuries and loss of motor and sensory function, an observation that remained clinically relevant for centuries. [6]

Influence and Legacy:

The Edwin Smith Papyrus is often regarded as a precursor to later medical works, including those of Hippocrates and Galen, though it predates these figures by over a millennium. The rational, scientific approach to medicine outlined in the papyrus is similar to the methods used in modern clinical practice, particularly in the field of trauma surgery. Its emphasis on diagnosis, prognosis, and treatment based on careful observation and empirical evidence represents a major milestone in the history of medicine.

The papyrus has been extensively studied since its translation by James Henry Breasted in 1930. Breasted'swork revolutionized the understanding of ancient Egyptian medicine, demonstrating that the Egyptians employed sophisticated surgical techniques and medical practices that were far more advanced than previously thought. Subsequent translations and studies, including a modern English translation by James P. Allen in 2006, have provided further insights into this remarkable document. [7, 8]

Conclusion:

The Edwin Smith Papyrus is an invaluable source of information on ancient Egyptian medical practices, particularly in the field of trauma and surgery. Its rational and scientific approach to diagnosing and treating injuries, combined with its detailed anatomical knowledge, showcases the Egyptians' advanced medical expertise. The text continues to be a vital resource for understanding the development of medicine in the ancient world and remains a testament to the skill and knowledge of Egyptian physicians.

Refrences:

1. Wilkins, Robert H. (1992) [First published 1965]. *Neurosurgical Classics* (2nd ed.). Park Ridge, Illinois: American Association of Neurological Surgeons. ISBN 978-1-879284-09-8. LCCN 2011293270.

2. Ghalioungui, Paul (1965) [First published 1963]. *Magic and Medical Science in Ancient Egypt*. New York: Barnes & Noble. LCCN 65029851.

3. Martin, Andrew J. (2005-07-27). "Academy Papyrus to be Exhibited at the Metropolitan Museum of Art" (Press release). The New York Academy of Medicine. Archived from the original on November 27, 2010. Retrieved 2015-06-03.

4. Allen, James P. (2005). *The Art of Medicine in Ancient Egypt*. New York/New Haven: The Metropolitan Museum of Art/Yale University Press. ISBN 978-0-300-10728-9. LCCN 2005016908

5. *The Edwin Smith surgical papyrus, published in facsimile and hieroglyphic transliteration with translation and commentary in two volumes* (PDF). Chicago, Ill.: University of Chicago, Oriental Institute. 1930. ISBN *978-0-918986-73-3*., fulltext of translation with commentary.

6. Ritner, Robert K. (2005) [First published 2001]. "Medicine". In Redford, Donald B. (ed.). *Archived copy. The Oxford Encyclopedia of Ancient Egypt* (Online ed.). Oxford Reference. ISBN 978-0-19-518765

6. LCCN 99054801. Archived from the original on 2016-08-17. Retrieved 2016-01-04.

7. Breasted, James Henry (1991) [First published 1930]. *The Edwin Smith Surgical Papyrus: published in facsimile and hieroglyphic transliteration with translation and commentary in two volumes*. University of Chicago Oriental Institute Publications, v. 3–4. Chicago: University of Chicago Press. ISBN 978-0-918986-73-3. LCCN 31007705.

8. Mandal, D. 2016. *Edwin Smith Papyrus: The World's Oldest Known Surgical Treatise, And Yet It Might Be ACopy!*. [Online] Available
at: https://www.realmofhistory.com/2016/12/07/edwin-smith-papyrus-oldest-surgical-treatise/

SUSHRUTA: THE FATHER OF SURGERY

A statue of Sushruta (600 BCE) at Royal

Australasian College of

Surgeons (RACS)

in Melbourne, Australia.[1]

Sushruta is recognized as one of the earliest and most important physicians and surgeons in the history of Ayurveda. He is often regarded as the "Father of Surgery" for his comprehensive contributions to the field of medical science, particularly surgery. Indian scholars date Sushruta to ancient times, while Western historians place him around the 5th century AD. Sushruta's expertise and his monumental work, the "*Sushruta Samhita*", demonstrate his unparalleled knowledge of both medicine and surgery. The text advises students to practice surgical techniques on objects resembling the human body or diseased parts. For example, incisions are recommended on squash (*Pushpaphala*), bottle gourd (*Alabu*), cucumber (*Trapusha*), leather bags filled with fluids, and the bladders of dead animals. [1]

Sushruta Samhita: A Medical Masterpiece

The *Sushruta Samhita* is one of the oldest and most foundational texts in Ayurveda, containing extensive discussions on every aspect of medicine. While it covers the theories and principles of treatment and medicinal practices, the distinguishing feature of this work is its extraordinary detail on surgery. [2]This focus on surgery is what sets *Sushruta Samhita* apart from other classical Ayurvedic texts, such as the *Charaka Samhita*.

The Importance of Surgery According to Sushruta

Sushruta believed that a well-rounded physician must be proficient not only in medical treatment but also in surgery. He emphasized that a physician lacking surgical expertise is like a bird with only one wing, unable to fully practice the healing arts. This conviction led him to include a significant section on surgical procedures, tools, and techniques in his work. His comprehensive and practical knowledge of surgery made *Sushruta Samhita* an essential text for practitioners of Ayurveda.

Surgical Knowledge in Sushruta Samhita

The Sushruta Samhita divides its surgical knowledge into five major sections under the title "*Shalya Tantra*", meaning the science of surgery. These sections are:

1. *Sutra Sthana* – The foundational principles of surgery, including descriptions of various surgical techniques.

2. *Nidana Sthana* – The diagnosis of diseases that may require surgical intervention.

3. *Sharira Sthana* – Detailed information about human anatomy, essential for surgical procedures.

4. *Chikitsa Sthana* – The treatment of diseases through surgical and non-surgical methods.

5. ***Kalpa Sthana*** – Focuses on toxicology and the treatment of poisoning.

In these sections, Sushruta describes over 100 types of surgical instruments, including their design and uses,resembling to the organs of animals and birds. These tools are remarkably similar to the modern instruments used today; demonstrating Sushruta's advanced understanding of surgery.

Sushruta classified surgery into seven main categories:

- ***Chedya*** (excision)
- ***Lekhya***(scarification)
- ***Vedhya*** (puncturing)
- ***Esya*** (exploration)
- ***Ahrya*** (extraction)
- ***Vsraya*** (evacuation)
- ***Sivya*** (suturing).

His writings emphasize key surgical principles like planning, precision, hemostasis, and perfection. Sushruta also detailed reconstructive procedures for various defects. In his seminal work, the Sushruta Samhita, he outlined 60 methods for wound treatment, described 120 surgical instruments, 300 surgical procedures, and classified surgeries into eight categories, marking a foundational contribution to the field of surgery. [3]

Sushruta's expertise extended to procedures like rhinoplasty (reconstruction of the nose), removal of foreign bodies, treating fractures, and even cataract surgery.Sushruta treated numerous cases of Nasa Sandhan (rhinoplasty), Oshtha Sandhan (lobuloplasty), and Karna Sandhan (otoplasty). His pioneering work in reconstructive surgery, especially rhinoplasty, which he described around 600 BCE, is still referred to as the Indian flap technique. Due to these advancements, Sushruta is widely regarded as the originator of **plastic surgery**. [3]

Sushruta's contributions to surgery are nothing short of groundbreaking, especially considering the time period in which he lived. His Sushruta Samhita not only outlines advanced surgical techniques but also provides practical descriptions of various medical tools and procedures. Here's a more detailed look at some of the surgical methods mentioned:

Ligature& Sutures (*Khayooti Jarahiya*)

Sushruta described various types of threads or sutures for stitching wounds, especially those resulting from accidents or injuries. These sutures were derived from both vegetable (such as jute fibers) and animal sources (such as hair). His innovation in using different materials for sutures reflects an early understanding of the importance of closing wounds to promote healing and prevent infections.

Skin Grafting (*Jild Peywandkari*) [4, 5, 6]

The Sushruta Samhita provides an advanced understanding of surgical techniques, particularly in the area of reconstructive surgery. It mentions several grafting methods, each with a distinct approach to repairing damaged or missing tissue:

- Sliding Graft

   This method involves sliding a portion of the skin from a nearby area to cover a wound or defect. It allows the surgeon to use healthy skin from an adjacent area, maintaining the tissue's connection to its blood supply, which is crucial for healing.

- Rotation Graft

   In this technique, a flap of skin is rotated from one part of the body to another. This method is particularly useful when the defect is located near the donor site of the graft, allowing for a more effective repair while ensuring the graft retains its blood supply.

- Pedicle Graft

The pedicle graft involves transferring skin from one part of the body to another while keeping a portion of the graft attached to its original blood supply. This ensures that the skin flap remains viable during the healing process, which was essential for successful reconstructive surgeries.

Rhinoplasty (Nose Reconstruction) [5]

One of the most remarkable techniques described in the Sushruta Samhita is rhinoplasty, the reconstruction of a nose that had been cut off. Sushruta's treatise records the earliest known cheek flap rhinoplasty, a technique still in use today. Sushruta's method involved using a flap of skin from the patient's cheek, which was shaped and then attached to the nasal area to form a new nose. This was particularly significant in ancient India, where cutting off a nose was sometimes a form of punishment. It describes over 15 methods for nose reconstruction, including the use of a cheek skin flap, remarkably similar to modern surgical approaches. Sushruta's technique not only restored physical appearance but also helped in restoring dignity to those who suffered such punishments.

Labioplasty[6]

The Sushruta Samhita also addresses labioplasty, a surgical procedure to reconstruct or repair the labia. This demonstrates Sushruta's concern with reconstructive surgeries in various parts of the body, emphasizing both functional and aesthetic aspects of the procedures.

Cystic Calculus (*Sang Masana*)[7]

Sushruta provided detailed descriptions of cystic calculus (bladder stones) and the surgical procedures to remove them. His work emphasizes diagnosis and intervention for this painful condition, demonstrating his understanding of both internal diseases and surgical remedies.

He listed **Six Varieties of Accidental Injuries:** [8, 9]

1. *Chinna* – Complete severance of a part or whole of a limb.
2. *Bhinna* – Deep injury to a hollow region caused by a long, piercing object.

3. ***Viddha Prana*** – Puncture of a structure that is not hollow.

4. ***Kshata*** – Uneven injuries showing signs of both *Chinna* and *Bhinna*; essentially a laceration.

5. ***Pichchita*** – Crushed injury resulting from a fall or heavy blow.

6. ***Ghrsta*** – Superficial abrasion of the skin.

Hernia (*Fataq*)

Various types of hernia and their surgical repairs are discussed extensively in the Sushruta Samhita. Hernias, which involve the protrusion of an organ or tissue through a weak spot in the muscles, were recognized and treated by Sushruta, showing his deep anatomical knowledge and surgical proficiency.

Cataract (*Nazool-ul-Maa*)

In the realm of eye diseases, Sushruta made significant advancements in treating cataracts. He described in detail the surgical procedure for replacing the lens, which was essentially an early form of cataract surgery. This technique is evidence of his surgical precision, as eye surgeries are among the most delicate.

Amputation

Sushruta also documented the method of amputation, a procedure used to remove infected or gangrenous limbs. This was a critical procedure in cases where an infection could spread to the rest of the body, and Sushruta emphasized the need for careful removal of diseased tissues to preserve the patient's life.

Cesarean Section (Birth through Surgery)

The Cesarean section, a method of delivering a baby by cutting through the abdomen, is also described in the Sushruta Samhita. This non-natural method of childbirth highlights Sushruta's understanding of obstetrics and surgery, showing that he was aware of ways to save both mother and child in complicated childbirth cases.

Marmas (Vital Points)

Sushruta identified specific vital points on the human body, which he called Marmas. These are areas where a deep wound could potentially be fatal. This concept of marmas is unique to Indian medicine, showing a sophisticated understanding of the body's vulnerability, particularly in terms of trauma and its effects on life.

Conclusion

The above techniques highlight Sushruta's mastery of surgical procedures, ranging from routine sutures to complex operations like skin grafting and cataract surgery. His ability to describe these processes in great detail proves why Sushruta is rightfully regarded as the Father of Surgery. His methods influenced not only the practice of surgery in India but also paved the way for surgical advancements worldwide.

Refrences:

1. Majno, Guido (February 1976). "The Healing Hand". *Plastic and Reconstructive Surgery*. 57 (2):230. doi:10.1097/00006534-197602000-00022. ISSN 0032 1052. S2CID 10270499.

2. Menon IA, Haberman HF (1969). "Dermatological writings of ancient India". *Med Hist*. **13** (4): 387–392. doi:10.1017/s0025727300014824. PMC 1033984. PMID 4899819.

3. Singh V. Sushruta: The father of surgery. Natl J Maxillofac Surg. 2017 Jan-Jun;8(1):1-3. doi: 10.4103/njms.NJMS_33_17. PMID: 28761269; PMCID: PMC5512402.

4. Lana Thompson. *Plastic Surgery*. ABC-CLIO. p. 8.

5. Melvin A. Shiffman, Alberto Di Gi. *Advanced Aesthetic Rhinoplasty: Art, Science, and New Clinical Techniques.* Springer Science & Business Media. p. 132.

6. Sharma, Kumar. *History BA (Programme) Semester II: Questions and Answers, University of Delhi.* Pearson Education India. p. 147.Lock etc., page 836

7. Engler, Steven (2003). "Science" vs." Religion" in Classical Ayurveda". *Numen.* **50** (4): 416-463.

8. Singh V. Sushruta: The father of surgery. Natl J Maxillofac Surg 2017;8:1-3. DOI: 10.4103/njms.NJMS_33_17

Medieval Islamic Surgeons: Their Innovations, Surgical Instruments, and Enduring Legacy

S.No	Name	Lifespan (CE)	Latinized Name	Notable Contributions
1	**Al-Razi**	0854 – 0925	Rhazes	Pioneer in clinical medicine; authored *Kitab al-Hawi*
2	**Ibn Al-Jazzar**	0895 – 0980	—	Known for *Zad al-Musafir* on travel and preventive medicine
3	**Al-Zahrawi**	0936 – 1013	Albucasis	Father of surgery; compiled surgical techniques in *Al-Tasrif*
4	**Ibn Sina**	0980 – 1037	Avicenna	Authored *Canon of Medicine*; integrated philosophy and healing
5	**Ibn Zuhr**	1091 – 1162	Avenzoar	Early clinical methods; first tracheotomy description
6	**Al-Baghdadi,**	1117 –	—	Compiled

S.No	Name	Lifespan (CE)	Latinized Name	Notable Contributions
	Muhadhdhab Al-Deen	1213		medical texts; philosopher-physician
7	**Ibn Rushd**	1125 – 1198	Averroes	Commentator on Aristotle; wrote *Kulliyat* on general medicine
8	**Al-Baghdadi, Muwafaq Al-Deen**	1162 – 1231	—	Known for contributions to materia medica
9	**Al-Dakhwar**	1170 – 1231	—	Court physician; teacher of surgery and medicine
10	**Ibn Abi Usaibiaa**	1204 – 1270	—	Authored *Uyūn al-Anbā ʾfīṬabaqāt al-Aṭibbāʾ* (history of medicine)
11	**Ibn Al-Nafis**	1210 – 1288	—	Discovered pulmonary circulation; challenged Galenic doctrine
12	**Ibn Al-Quff**	1232 – 1286	—	Surgeon; authored *Al-ʿUmdafi'l-Jirāḥa* (The Mainstay in Surgery)

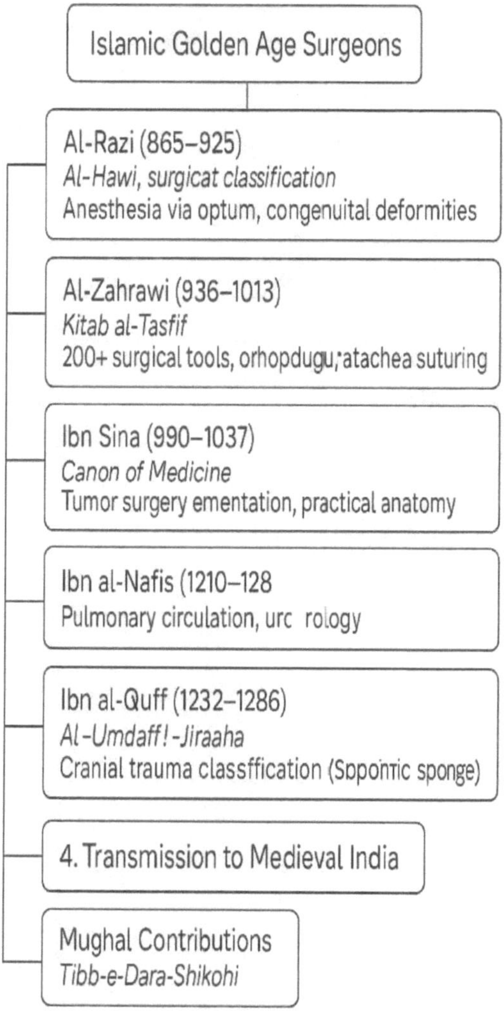

Islamic Golden Age Surgeons

Al-Razi (865–925)
Al-Hawi, surgicat classification
Anesthesia via optum, congenuital deformities

Al-Zahrawi (936–1013)
Kitab al-Tasfif
200+ surgical tools, orhopdugu;atachea suturing

Ibn Sina (990–1037)
Canon of Medicine
Tumor surgery ementation, practical anatomy

Ibn al-Nafis (1210–128
Pulmonary circulation, urc rology

Ibn al-Quff (1232–1286)
Al-Umdaff!-Jiraaha
Cranial trauma classffication (Sopoɴᴛɪᴄ sponge)

4. Transmission to Medieval India

Mughal Contributions
Tibb-e-Dara-Shikohi

AL Razi

Abū Bakr al-Rāzī, also known as **Rhazes** [a] (full name: أبو بكر محمد بن زكرياء الرازي, *Abū Bakr Muḥammad ibn Zakariyyā᾽ al-Rāzī*),[b] c. 864 or 865–925 or 935 CE, was a Persian physician, philosopher and alchemist who lived during the Islamic Golden Age. A comprehensive thinker, al-Razi made fundamental and enduring contributions to various fields, which he recorded in over 200 manuscripts, and is particularly remembered for numerous advances in medicine through his observations and discoveries. [1]

Al-Razi's Contributions to Surgery (Scientific Summary) [2, 3]

Clinical Compilation and Surgical Knowledge (via Al-Hawi):

o *Al-Hawi* (The Comprehensive Book on Medicine), a 23-volume text, compiled surgical knowledge from Greek, Indian, and Islamic sources.

o Included **empirical observations and personal clinical experience** related to:

- Wound care and abscess drainage
- Tumor identification and treatment (oncology)
- Management of fractures and dislocations
- Gynecological and obstetric surgical procedures
- Ophthalmic surgery techniques

Scientific Surgical Techniques:

o Detailed **operative procedures** such as:

- Bladder stone extraction
- Hernia treatment
- Abscess incision and drainage

o Stressed **asepsis (cleanliness)** and **post-operative care,** anticipating modern principles of infection control.

Emphasis on Clinical Observation and Experimentation:

o Advocated **experimental medicine**—using observation, diagnosis, and follow-up.

o One of the earliest to apply **case documentation** and outcome evaluation in surgical settings.

Development of Anesthesia:

o First physician known to **prepare and administer opium as a surgical anesthetic**.

o Enabled surgical procedures to be performed with **pain relief and patient stability**, a major advance in operative care.

Refinement of Distillation Techniques:

o While Jabir Ibn Hayyan introduced the basic concept of distillation, **Al-Razi advanced and perfected the technique** and improved **chemical distillation methods**, allowing for:

- Extraction and purification of **medicinal substances**

- Preparation of antiseptics, analgesics, and surgical compounds.

Influence on Later Medical Traditions:

o His works, especially *Al-Mansuri*'s *On Surgery*, were **translated into Latin** and became part of European medical curricula.

o Influenced renowned Islamic surgeons like **Al-Zahrawi** and **Ibn Zuhr**, who expanded upon his experimental and clinical approach.

Surgery for Congenital Deformities According to al-Razi

- **Cleft Lip**

o Al-Razi recognized cleft lip as a congenital deformity that could be surgically corrected.

o He included it under cosmetic surgery, which he considered a valid and important branch of surgical practice.

- **Tied Tongue (Ankyloglossia)**

o Described procedures to sever the lingual frenulum, improving speech and oral mobility.

- **Blocked Ears**

o Al-Razi detailed techniques to clear obstructions in the ear canal, enhancing hearing.

- **Finger Deformities**

o Polydactyly: Advised removal of extra fingers through surgery.
o Syndactyly: Recommended separation of fused fingers to restore function and appearance.

- **Eyelid Deformity (Ectropion)**

o Identified ectropion (outward turning of the eyelid) and suggested surgical correction.

- **Siamese Twins**

o While not specifically mentioned by al-Razi, historical accounts note that Muslim surgeons attempted separation surgeries if the fusion was superficial and operable.

Al-Razi's integration of **scientific rigor, experimental methodology, pharmacology, and ethical surgical**

practice marks him as a foundational figure in the history of surgery, both in the Islamic world and medieval Europe.

References:

1.   Hakeem Abdul Hameed, <u>Exchanges between India and Central Asia in the field of Medicine</u> Archived 6 October 2008 at the <u>Wayback Machine</u>

2.   "Ar-Razi (Rhazes), 864–930 C.E." *www.unhas.ac.id. Archived from the original on 20 February 2020.* Retrieved 27 February 2020. *Ar-Razi was a pioneer in many areas of medicine and treatment and the health sciences in general. In particular, he was a pioneer in the fields of pediatrics, obstetrics and ophthalmology.*

3.   Phipps, Claude (5 October 2015). No Wonder You Wonder!: Great Inventions and Scientific Mysteries. Springer. p. 111. ISBN 9783319216805.

Al-Zahrawi (936-1013)

Born c. 936. Medina Azahara, al-Andalus
(near present-day Córdoba, Spain)
Died 1013 (aged 76–77)
Occupation Physician
Known for Pioneer of surgery
Author of medical encyclopedia *Kitab al-Tasrif* [1, 2]

Biography

Abul Qasim Khalaf ibn al-Abbas al-Zahrawi, (Arabic: أبو القاسم خلف بن العباس الزهراوي) known in the West as Abulcasis or Albucasis, was a prominent 10th-century surgeon born in al-Zahra, near Cordoba, Spain in 936AD.[1, 2] He belonged to the Ansar tribe from Medina and lived most ofhis life in Cordoba, where he served as a court physician to the Umayyad caliphs Abd al-Rahman III and Al-Hakam II.[3]His medical knowledge and innovations, particularly in surgery, were groundbreaking, including the use of catgut for stitches and the development of surgical instruments for procedures like Caesarean sections and cataract surgeries. His major work, *Kitab al-Tasrif*, became a medical reference in Europe for centuries, influencing both Eastern and Western medicine. [4] Al-Zahrawi is also credited with identifying hemophilia and describing abdominal pregnancies. He passed away in 1013 AD, leaving a lasting legacy in the field of surgery. [5]

Surgical Career

Al-Zahrawi's contributions to surgery are among the most groundbreaking in the history of medicine, particularly in the medieval Islamic world. He specialized in cauterization, a method where heat is used to burn and seal off wounds or stop bleeding. This technique was applied across many conditions to manage infections and control hemorrhages, a common practice in his time, but he elevated its use by refining the technique and developing new tools.

Innovations in Surgical Instruments:

Al-Zahrawi was a prolific inventor of surgical instruments. He designed several devices that greatly expanded the scope of surgical intervention, including tools for:

- Inspection of internal body organs, such as the urethra, throat, and ear.

- Removal of foreign bodies from sensitive areas like the ear canal and throat, improving the treatment of obstructions or infections.

- He also developed various cannulae, which are thin tubes inserted into the body to allow fluid drainage or to administer fluids. Al-Zahrawi was the first to illustrate the design and use of such instruments, which are still foundational in modern surgery.

- First Use of Caustic Metal and Iron Tubes:Al-Zahrawi pioneered the use of iron tubes and caustic metals to treat warts and other skin conditions. This involved using an iron tube as a guide for applying caustic substances directly to warts, burning them off with precision. This method of localized cauterization was revolutionary for its time, as it allowed for effective treatment without damaging surrounding healthy tissue.[6]

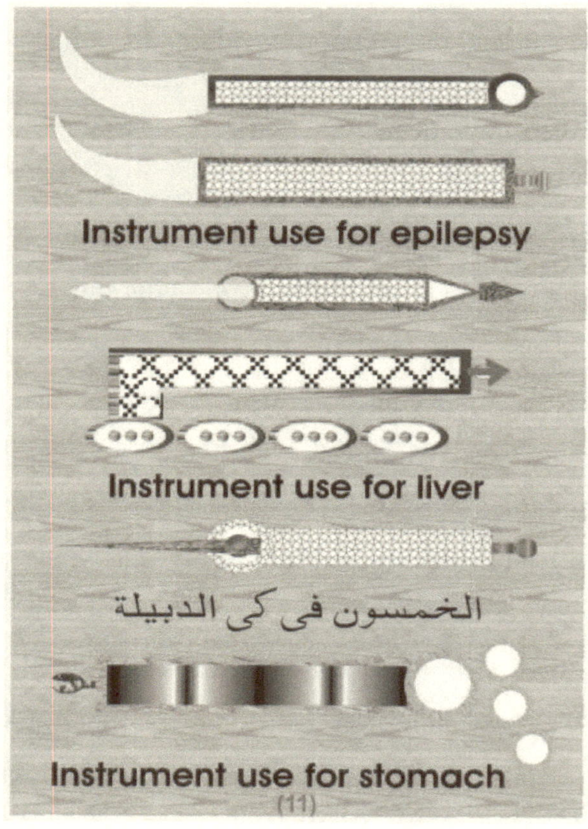

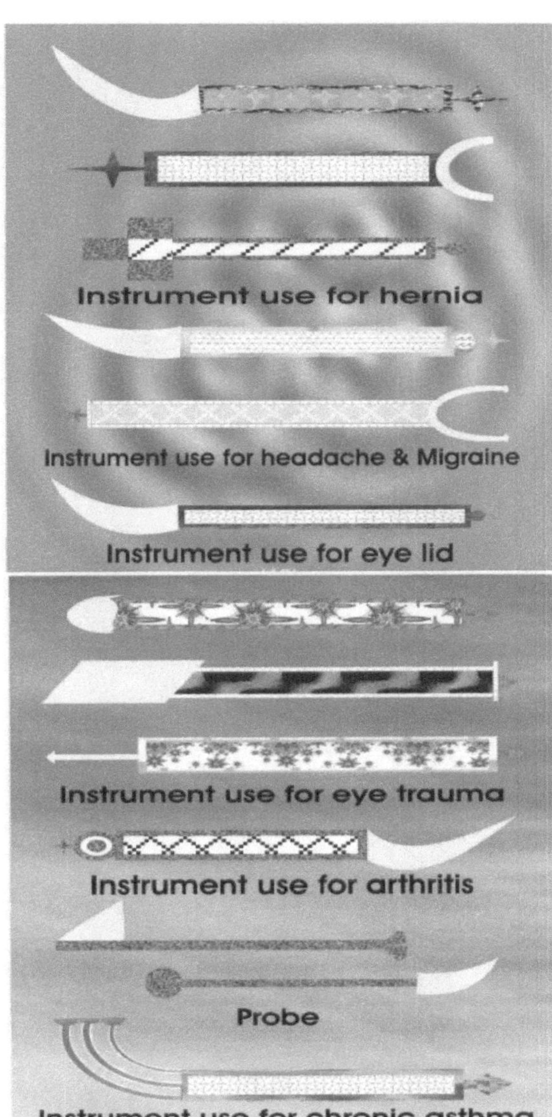

Instrument use for hernia
Instrument use for headache & Migraine
Instrument use for eye lid
Instrument use for eye trauma
Instrument use for arthritis
Probe
Instrument use for chronic asthma

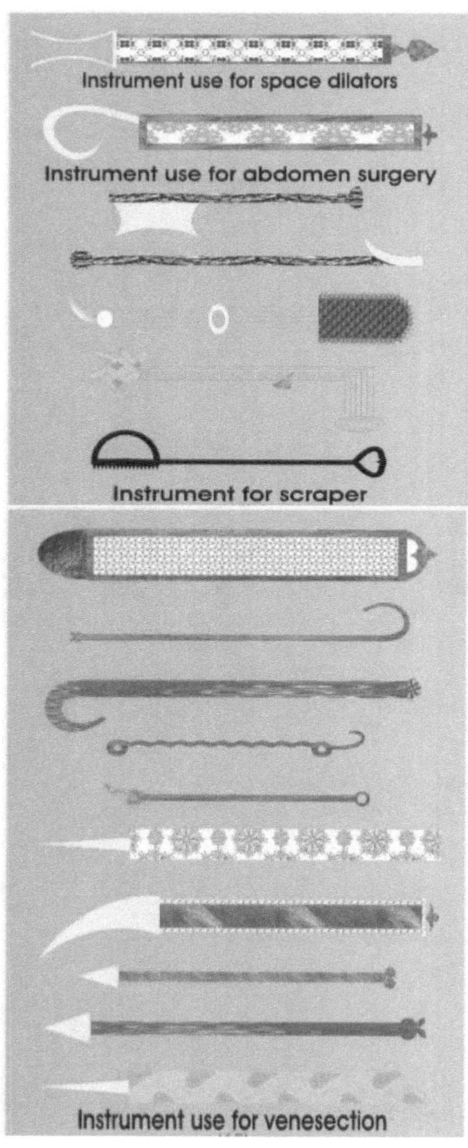

Instrument use for space dilators
Instrument use for abdomen surgery
Instrument for scraper
Instrument use for venesection

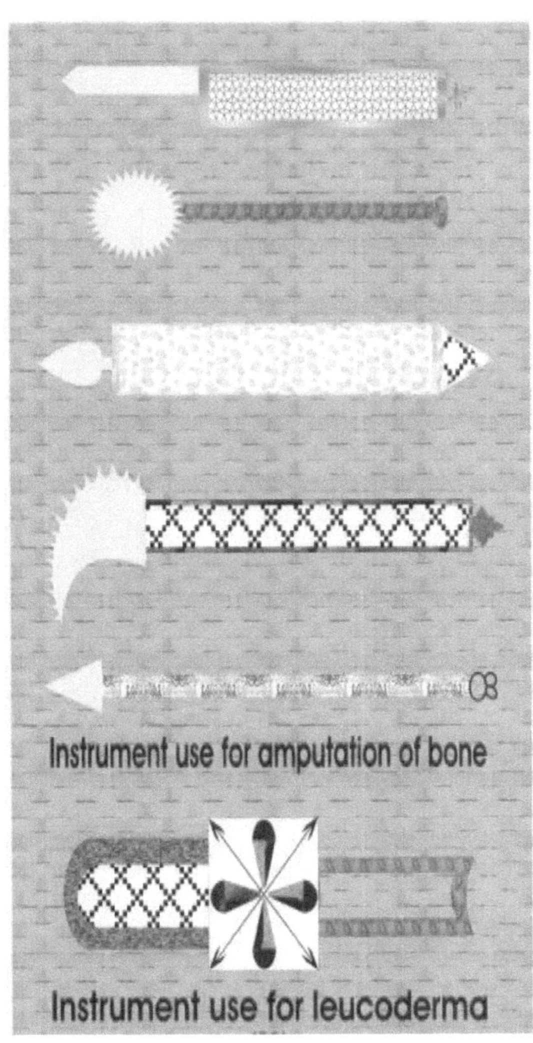

Instrument use for amputation of bone
Instrument use for leucoderma

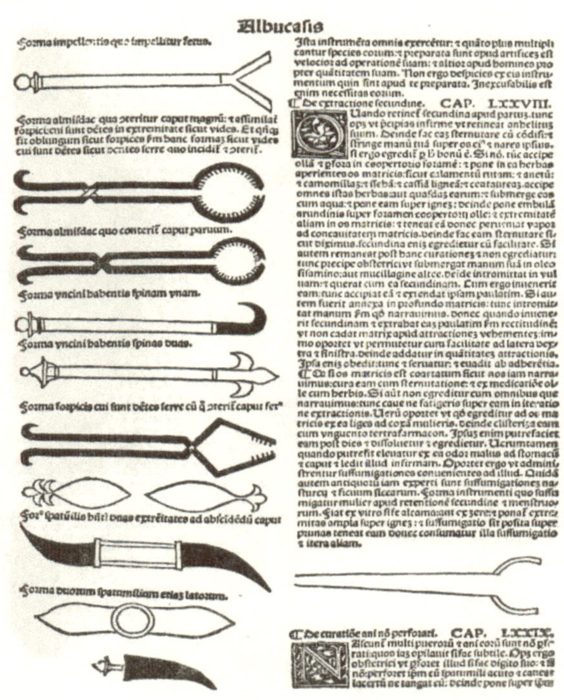

Surgical instruments described by al-Zahrawi. Line illustration Wellcome Images Keywords: History of Medicine; medicine, islamic; Albucasis Scalpels. Rare Books Keywords: Instruments;Albucasis.(https://upload.wikimedia.org/wikipedia/commons/thumb/9/96/Albucasis%2C_Chirurgia_Albucasum%2C_14th_C_Wellcome_M0004106.jpg/800px

Neurosurgical Pioneering:

Al-Zahrawi also made significant strides in neurosurgery and neurological diagnosis. He treated a variety of head and spinal injuries that were poorly understood at the time. His work in this specialization is described below:

Head injuries and skull fractures: Al-Zahrawi treated patients with head trauma, performing surgeries to repair skull fractures, which was an advanced practice at the time. Abulcasis' groundbreaking work on head injuries and skull fractures:

> 1. Classified fractures into penetrating and crushing types.
> 2. Described "ping-pong" fractures in children, likening them to dents in a bronze bowl.
> 3. Identified ominous signs indicating poor prognosis, such as vomiting, seizures, and loss of speech.
> 4. Recommended surgical intervention, including shaving the scalp and removing bone fragments.

5. Al-Zahrawi provided one of the earliest and most comprehensive surgical techniques for treating cranial injuries involving abscesses or hemorrhage.

The procedure began with cleansing the affected area using wine and rose oil, both known for their antiseptic properties. Once bleeding had ceased and it was safe to proceed, typically within 7 days in summer or 14 days in winter, the surgeon would begin removing the damaged bone.

He introduced the use of specially designed "non-sinking" drills, which featured a circular collar beneath the cutting edge to prevent them from penetrating too deeply and damaging the delicate membrane beneath the skull. The surgeon would use these drills to make multiple perforations around the injured area, spacing them about the width of a surgical probe. Once the bone was weakened by these holes, chisels were used delicately to cut beneath the perforations. The loosened bone was then carefully lifted out using the hand, forceps, or fine tongs—always with great caution to avoid contact with the underlying membrane.

After the bone was removed, any rough or uneven edges were smoothed with a slender, chisel-like instrument. Al-Zahrawi emphasized the importance of precision and gentleness throughout the procedure to avoid further injury. Following surgery, he advised dressing the wound with clean linen soaked in wine and rose oil to promote healing and prevent infection. This technique reflected a remarkably advanced understanding of neurosurgery, antisepsis, and post-operative care for his time.[7]

Spinal injuries: Abulcasis had a rather extensive discussion of spinal injuries and fractures [12:812-9]. Methods of immobilization and traction were described. He noted, how-ever:

"WHEN ANY OF THE VERTEBRAE OF THE BACK OR NECK ARE COMPLETELY DISLOCATED OR A NUMBER OF VERTEBRAE ARE DISPLACED, THERE IS NO TREATMENT IN THIS CASE, FOR DEATH IS HASTENING TOWARD THE PATIENT. THE SIGN OF THIS IS THAT THE INJURED MAN PASSES A MOTION INVOLUNTARILY, BEING UNABLE TO HOLD IT BACK; OFTEN TOO SOME OF HIS LIMBS GO LIMP, EITHER BOTH LEGS OR BOTH ARMS OR ONE OF THEM."

Al-Zahrawi dedicated a special chapter to the treatment of fractured and dislocated vertebrae in the back and neck. He wrote as follows: "When a fracture occurs in the bones of the neck, which is rare, as they usually suffer contusions, and the same applies to spinal vertebrae in general, to determine whether the injury will heal or not, observe the hands. If both hands are relaxed, numb, and lifeless, with no ability to move, stretch, or close them, and the patient does not respond to pinching or pricking with a needle, it is a general rule that the injury will not heal and the patient is doomed. However, if the patient can move both hands and feels the pinching or pricking, this indicates that the spinal cord (medulla) remains intact, and with treatment, the patient will recover. Al-Zahrawi further explained that if a similar injury occurs to the vertebrae of the back and you wish to determine whether the patient will recover, focus on the feet. If the feet appear relaxed and lifeless, as described in the case of the hands, the prognosis is likely hopeless. Additionally, he noted that two other severe signs in back injuries included the involuntary passage of gas and feces, as well as involuntary urination while lying prone or an inability to urinate while lying on the back. These signs indicated a poor prognosis. [7]

Subdural effusions and headaches: His work extended to other neurological conditions, such as the treatment of subdural effusions (a collection of fluid between the brain and skull) and severe headaches, which might now be recognized as forms of intracranial pressure or even early descriptions of migraines.[2]

Hydrocephalus: One of his most notable contributions was in the treatment of hydrocephalus (a condition involving an accumulation of fluid in the brain). Al-Zahrawi provided the first known clinical description of an operative procedure for hydrocephalus in children. He described the drainage of intracranial fluid, a concept that laid the foundation for modern neurosurgical procedures like ventriculo-peritoneal shunting, which is still used today to treat hydrocephalus.[2]

Facial palsy and Cauterization: Abulcasis' surgical thesis extensively covers cauterization methods, a common treatment approach in the Middle Ages. Cauterization was used to address various conditions, including paralysis,

epilepsy, tremors, and numbness. The technique involved applying heat to specific areas, such as the shaved head or vertebral spinous processes. For limb numbness, cauterization targeted the spinous process near the nerve exit. Abulcasis emphasized the importance of anatomical knowledge for effective treatment. Notably, he treated facial palsy by cauterizing the unaffected side of the face to balance facial tone, applying cauterization at specific sites like the root of the ear or temple area. This approach demonstrates his understanding of nerve function and anatomy.

Ear Nose Throat Surgery:

For tracheostomy he said: 'Count three or four rings of the windpipe and cut the membrane lying between two cartilages and then attach the cartilages to the skin'.

For tonsillectomy he said: 'Depress the tongue by means of a tool, then insert a hook in the tonsil and pull it outwards and then cut it by means of strong scissors'.

Al-Zahrawi was able to perform ear surgeries like incongenital aural atresia, scar and stenosis after injury, or polyps and granulation, extracting the foreign bodies.

Al-Zahrawi talked about nose surgery like Nasal Fila Operation, Nasal Polyps Tumors, Nasal Fractures etc.

**Case of the
Slave Girl: Surgical Suturing of the Trachea.** [1]

Though Al-Zahrawi did not perform tracheotomies, his clinical case report of a slave girl who attempted suicide by cutting her throat was a significant advancement in surgical knowledge. The girl had severed part of her trachea, which would have been considered a fatal injury at the time. Upon examination, Al-Zahrawi noted that while the trachea had been cut, neither a major artery nor the jugular vein was damaged. Air escaped through the wound, but there was minimal bleeding. He sutured the wound, and remarkably, the girl recovered, with only slight hoarseness remaining. This case demonstrated for the first time that an incision in the larynx could heal with proper treatment, challenging the prevailing belief that such injuries were universally fatal. His success in this case contributed to the future development of tracheotomy and other throat surgeries. [12]

In Orthopedic surgery:

- He presented what is called today Kocher's technique for decrease of shoulder disengagement and patelectomy, 1,000 years before Brooke reintroduced it in 1937.

- He depicted tracheotomy, orthodontia and portrayed the distinctive sorts of crack before the presentation of X Rays.

- American surgeon W.S. Halsted (1922) has opined that Zahrawi was the first surgeon to have done thyroid operation.

- Among some treatments used by him, was the reduction of fractured bones: "...the broken bone had to be splinted, extended and adjusted, and if this was not sufficient an incision was made at the end of the bone, and a branch of fir was inserted into the cavity of the medulla..." Modern medicine developed a technique similar to this in the 20th century known as medullary fixation.

Eye Surgery:

El Zahrawi described an operation for treating entropion, trichiasis which is probably as efficient as the method popular nowadays.

- He removed a wedge of skin from the eyelid, then made a release incision in the conjunctiva, and then sutured the skin edges together. In this way the edge of the eyelid is rotated outwards over the edge of the tarsal plate, carrying the hairs away from eyeball.

He describes the treatment of pterygium as follows:

- "Insert a needle under the pterygium and raise it. Then insert a horse-tail hair under it and saw off the part lying outside the cornea by moving the hair sideways. Then remove the part on the cornea with a sharp, smooth blade".

These are El Zahrawi's own words and this is almost exactly the operation used now (but not with a horse hair of course). Hypopion was treated by incision in the limbus and drainage.

DENTISTRY:

Al-Zahrawi made the most notable contributions to dentistry and periodontics among Muslim physicians.

- He devised various types of forceps for extraction of teeth and described the fixation of loose teeth by wire made of gold or silver, and has been credited as the first to perform tooth replantation in dental history.[8, 9]

- He designed tools for scaling dental calculus, promoting it as a preventive measure against periodontal disease.

- He suggested the use of animal bones for making false teeth. [10, 11]

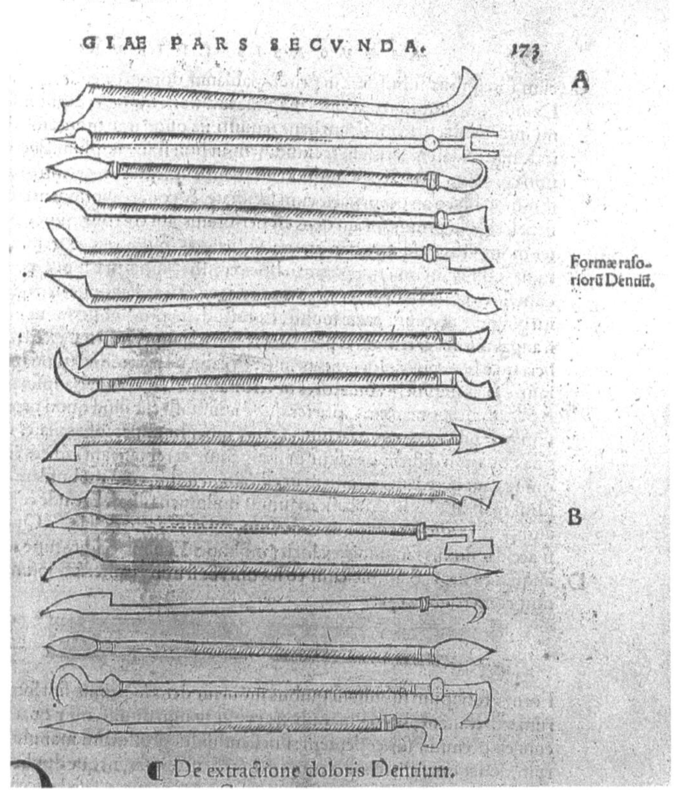

Albucasishttps://en.wikipedia.org/wiki/File:Dental_instr
uments,_from_%27Chirurgia%27_Wellcome_L00168
68.jpg

Breast Surgery:

Al Zahrawi described two different surgical techniques
for the treatment of gynecomastia. [12]

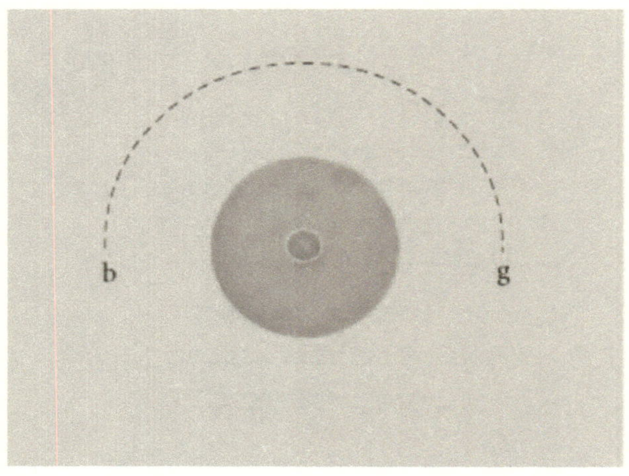

Figure a: Surgical treatment of moderate gynaecomastia according to Al-Zahrawi. A lunate incision is made above the breast and the subcutaneous fat is removed (points b and g delimit the incision).[12]

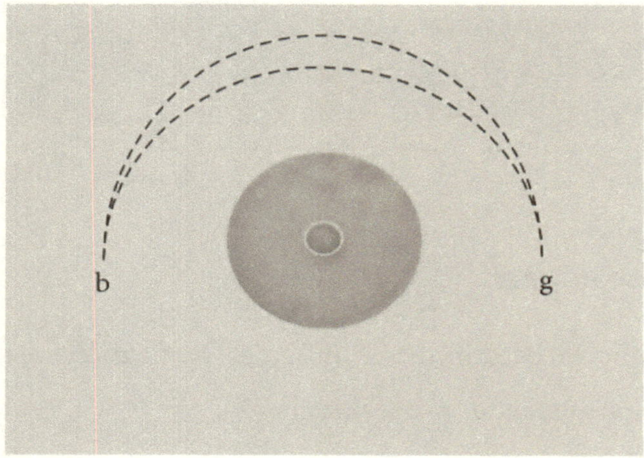

Figure b: Surgical treatment of severe gynaecomastia according to Al-Zahrawi. Two lunate incisions are made along the upper part of the breast to allow the removal of subcutaneous fat along with the excess skin (points b and g delimit the incision).[12]

From *Kitabultasrif*:

In the medieval era, Al-Zahrawi made significant advancements in the surgical treatment of gynecomastia by describing two distinct techniques. Unlike the Greco-Roman physician Paulus of Aegina, who recommended making incisions below the breast, Al-Zahrawi suggested making a lunate (crescent-shaped) incision above the breast. This approach not only allowed for the effective removal of subcutaneous fat but may have also provided better aesthetic results by offering a mild breast lift. He also introduced the use of cicatrizing or flesh-regenerating substances—such as dragon's blood (Calamus draco)—to promote wound healing, which marked a notable departure from previous practices and highlighted his understanding of medicinal plants and pharmacology.

In more severe cases of gynecomastia, Al-Zahrawi described a second technique involving two lunate incisions along the upper part of the breast. This allowed the surgeon to remove both fat and excess skin. After the procedure, he recommended applying a styptic powder to control bleeding and accelerate healing. These powders were composed of natural substances like aloe vera, dragon's blood, gum Arabic, sarcocolla, and myrrh—many of which have since been validated by modern medicine for their antimicrobial and wound-healing properties. Al-Zahrawi's detailed surgical guidance and use of therapeutic agents reflect a sophisticated integration of surgical skill and pharmacological knowledge well ahead of his time.[12]

Urology:

In the field of urology, Al-Zahrawi made a groundbreaking contribution by developing a less invasive method for removing bladder stones. He invented an early version of the lithotrite, which he named the "Michaab," allowing him to crush stones within the bladder without making a surgical incision. This innovation significantly reduced the pain and risk associated with traditional European lithotomy methods of the time, which were often extremely painful and carried a high risk of death. His technique marked a major advancement in urological surgery and laid the foundation for more refined and safer procedures in the centuries that followed.[13]

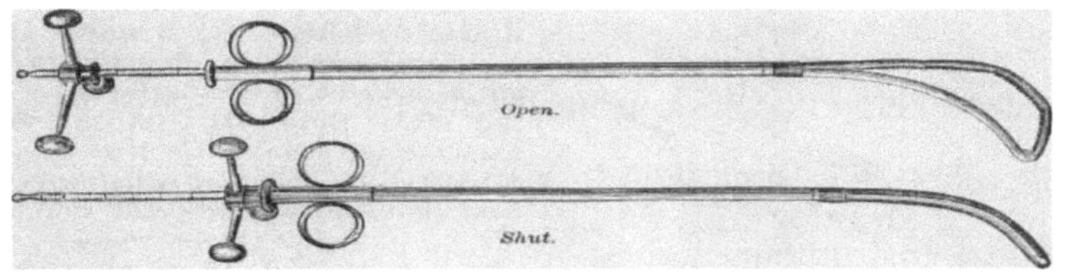

An early lithotrite "*Michaab*" showing the device in open and closed positions [13]

OBSTETRICS:

Al Zahrawi was the first to describe 'Walcher's position' for difficult labour and 'Cred's method' for extraction of the retained placenta.

Al-Zahrawi also developed a specialized forceps for removing a deceased fetus, a tool he illustrated in his medical encyclopedia *Kitab al-Tasrif*.[14]

Around 1000 AD, he wrote his famous book "*Al Tasreef Liman 'Ajaz 'Aan Al-Taleef*", (The Clearance of Medical Science For Those Who Can Not Compile It), a 30-volume medical encyclopedia summarizing 50 years of experience. It covered medicine, surgery, midwifery, pharmacology, dietetics, psychotherapy, and medical chemistry.[15]

Broader Impact on Surgery:

Al-Zahrawi's legacy lies in the vast scope of his surgical contributions, which influenced both the East and West for centuries. His magnum opus, *Kitab al-Tasrif*, especially its chapters on surgery, was translated into Latin and became a standard reference in European medical schools for over 500 years. His detailed illustrations and descriptions of surgical instruments, techniques, and case studies helped disseminate his knowledge far beyond Andalusia, where he practiced. His instruments and techniques, including the use of catgut for internal stitches, are still part of modern surgical practice.

In essence, Al-Zahrawi was not only a surgeon but also a medical innovator whose work bridged traditional medical practices and the beginnings of what would evolve into modern surgery. His meticulous attention to detail, his ability to develop new surgical methods and tools, and his pioneering treatments in the fields of both general and neurosurgery made him one of the greatest surgeons in medical history. His work remains influential to this day, demonstrating his profound understanding of anatomy, pathology, and surgical intervention.

References:

1. M. S. Spink and G. L. Lewis, *Albucasis on Surgery and Instruments*, Wellcome Institute of the History of Medicine,London, UK, 1973.

2. H. R. Al zahrawi, "Father of surgery," *Heart Views*, vol. 7, pp. 154–156, 2006.

3. R. F. Albucasis, *(Abu Al-Qasim Al-Zahrawi): Renowned Muslim Surgeon of the Tenth Century*, The Rosen PublishingGroup, New York, NY, USA, 2006.

4. Al-Zahrāwī, Abū al-Qāsim Khalaf ibn 'Abbās; Studies, Gustave E. von Grunebaum Center for Near Eastern (1973). *Albucasis on surgery and instruments*. University of California Press. ISBN 978-0-520-01532-6.

5. Cosman, Madeleine Pelner; Jones, Linda Gale (2008). *Handbook to Life in the Medieval World*. Handbook to Life Series. Vol. 2. Infobase Publishing. pp. 528–530. ISBN 978-0-8160-4887-8.

6.Missori, Paolo; Brunetto, Giacoma M.; Domenicucci, Maurizio (7 February 2012). "Origin of the Cannula for Tracheotomy During the Middle Ages and Renaissance". *World Journal of Surgery*. 36 (4): 928–934. doi:10.1007/s00268-012-1435-1. PMID 22311135. S2CID 3121262.

7. Al-Rodhan NR, Fox JL. Al-Zahrawi and Arabian neurosurgery, 936–1013 AD. Surgical neurology. 1986 Jul 1;26(1):92-5.

8. Becker, Marshall Joseph; Turfa, Jean MacIntosh (2017). The Etruscans and the History of Dentistry: The Golden Smile Through the Ages. Taylor & Francis. p. 146.

9. Ingle, John Ide; Baumgartner, J. Craig (2008). Ingle's Endodontics. PMPH-USA. p. 1281."The individual first credited

with the principle of extraction and replantation was an Arabian physician by the name of Abulcasis who practiced in the eleventh century."

10. Ingle, John Ide; Bakland, Leif K. (2002). Endodontics. PMPH-USA. p. 727."Abulcasis, an Arabian physician practicing in the eleventh century, is the first credited with recording the principle of extraction/replantation."

11. Andrews, Esther K. (2007). Practice Management for Dental Hygienists. Lippincott Williams & Wilkins. p. 6."Abu al-Qasim, also known as Abulcasis, wrote an encyclopedia of medicine and surgery (al-Tasrif) that is now kept at Oxford University. His unique contribution to dentistry reported the relationship between calculus and periodontal disease. He promoted prevention by recommending scaling calculus above and below the gums until all accretions were removed even if it takes multiple visits."

12. Chavoushi SH, Ghabili K, Kazemi A, Aslanabadi A, Babapour S, Ahmedli R, Golzari SE. Surgery for Gynecomastia in the Islamic Golden Age: Al-Tasrif of Al-Zahrawi (936–1013 AD). International Scholarly Research Notices. 2012;2012(1):934965.

13. Butt, Arthur J. (1956). Etiologic Factors in Renal Lithiasis. Thomas. ISBN 978-0-398-04374-2.

14. Ingrid Hehmeyer and Aliya Khan (2007). "Islam's forgotten contributions to medical science", Canadian Medical Association Journal 176 (10).

15.Hamarneh S. Al-Zahrawi, Abul-Qasim Khalaf Ibn Abbas. In: Gillispie Charles Coulston., editor. Dictionary of Scientific Biography. XIV. Charles Scribner's Sons Publishers; New York: 1976. pp. 584–585. [Google Scholar]

Kitab al-Tasrif

The *Kitab al-Tasrif* remains one of the most influential works in medical history, laying the foundation for many modern surgical techniques and advancing medical knowledge across the globe.

Frontispiece of the Latin translation of al-*Kitab al-Tasrif*.
Two pages from the Arabic manuscript of the *Kitab al-Tasrif*.
Middle East, 13th century, Chester Beatty Library.[1]

Al-Zahrawi'sKitab al-Tasrif: Key Contributions to Medicine and Surgery

Monumental Medical Encyclopedia: [1] Al-Zahrawi's*Kitab al-Tasrif*, completed in 1000 AD, is a 30-volume encyclopedia covering a wide range of medical disciplines including surgery, medicine, orthopedics, ophthalmology, pharmacology, nutrition, dentistry, childbirth, and pathology.

Surgery as the Pinnacle of Medicine: [2] The final volume is entirely dedicated to surgery, which Al-Zahrawi regarded as the most refined medical art, requiring deep knowledge of all other branches.

Anatomy as a Prerequisite: [2] In the introduction, Al-Zahrawi stressed the critical importance of anatomy for physicians, especially surgeons. He insisted on understanding the structure and function of organs, muscles, bones, and tendons—crediting Hippocrates and Galen for this foundational emphasis.

Dangers of Ignorance in Surgery: [2] He illustrated the perils of surgical ignorance through the story of an untrained doctor who fatally severed arterieswhile treating a neck tumor, underscoring the need for anatomical precision.

Classification of Surgeries: [3]

Surgical procedures were categorized as either safe or high-risk, with Al-Zahrawi urging caution and thorough preparation before attempting any operation.

Advances in Neurosurgery:

He made significant contributions to brain and spinal surgery, detailing procedures like skull drilling and noting complications from cranial and spinal injuries.

Pioneering Techniques: [4, 5]

- Described methods akin to Kocher's technique for shoulder dislocation centuries before Kocher.

- Introduced the Walcher position in obstetrics.

- Detailed the ligation of blood vessels, centuries before Ambroise Paré.

- First to describe ligation of the temporal artery for migraines—a technique revived in the 21st century.

Insights into Genetics and Hemophilia:

Al-Zahrawi explained the hereditary nature of hemophilia long before modern genetic science.

Influence on Europe: [6]

After its Latin translation by Gerard of Cremona in the 12th century, *Kitab al-Tasrif* became Europe's premier surgical textbook, even surpassing Avicenna's *Canon of Medicine* in authority.

Structure of the Surgical Text: [7]
The surgical section was divided into:

- o Cauterization
- o Incision, perforation, venesection, and wound care
- o Bone-setting

  These were based on both Greek sources and Al-Zahrawi's personal experiences.

Illustrated Surgical Instruments:
Nearly 200 surgical tools were carefully illustrated and explained—many designed by Al-Zahrawi himself—making *Kitab al-Tasrif* the first illustrated surgical manual.

Legacy in the Islamic and Western World: [8]
Ottoman surgeon ŞerafeddinSabuncuoğlu translated and expanded the text in the 15th century, preserving and enhancing its legacy in both the Islamic world and Europe.

On Surgery and Instruments (Volume 30 of Kitab al-Tasrif) [9, 10, 11]

First Illustrated Surgical Manual: This volume is considered the most influential part of *Kitab al-Tasrif*, offering practical, illustrated guidance on surgical procedures and tools.

Bridge Between Theory and Practice: By combining textual instruction with detailed diagrams, Al-Zahrawi created a hands-on guide for surgeons, making surgical learning more accessible and effective.

Wide Range of Surgeries Covered: The volume included surgeries from simple incisions to complex orthopedic procedures and cauterizations, intended for both students and practicing surgeons.

Translation and European Impact: Translated into Latin by Gerard of Cremona, it became foundational in medical education at institutions like Salerno and Montpellier, dominating surgical practice in Europe for over 500 years.

Authoritative Status in Surgery: Historian Arturo Castiglioni noted that *On Surgery and Instruments* was to surgery what Avicenna's *Canon* was to general medicine—an unmatched medical authority.

Innovation and Pedagogy: Al-Zahrawi emphasized clarity, simplicity, and educational value. His illustrations and step-by-step guidance served not only as reference but as a teaching tool.

Foundation in Study and Experience: Al-Zahrawi combined deep scholarly reading with lifelong hands-on experience. He was dedicated to refining medical knowledge and presenting it without unnecessary complexity for future generations.

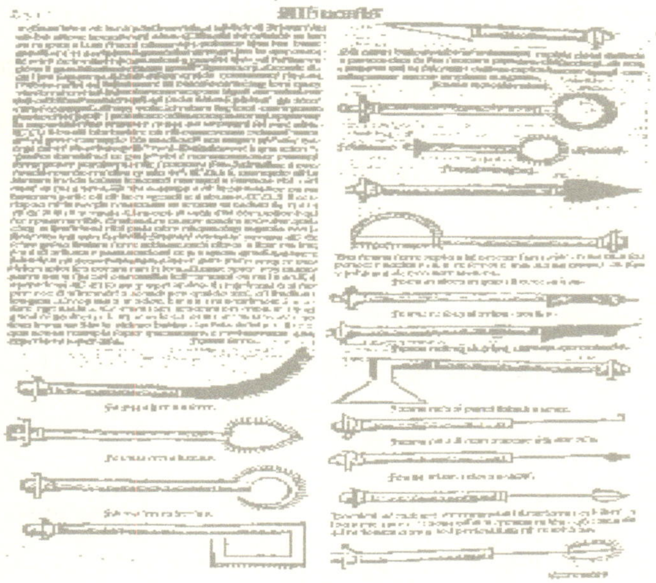

Page from a 1531 Latin translation by Peter Argellata of Al-Zahrawi's treatise on surgical and medical instruments.[9, 10, 11]

References:

1. "Theoretical and Practical Book by Al-Zahrawi. 1519.

2. KhudaBaksch Library Patna has two manuscripts of *al-Tasrif*, dated 1710 and 1888.Arabic edition was published in Lucknow 1908

3.M.S. Spink, Abulcasis: *On Surgery and Instruments*, London 1973- Wellcome Institute for History of Medicine. Available online:

https://books.google.ca/books?id=mjVra87nRScC&pg=PR5&redir_esc=y#v=onepage&q&f=false

4. Cosman, Madeleine Pelner; Jones, Linda Gale (2008). *Handbook to Life in the Medieval World*. Handbook to Life Series. Vol. 2. Infobase Publishing. pp. 528–530. ISBN 978-0-8160-4887-8.

5. Shevel, E; Spierings, EH (April 2004). "Role of the extracranial arteries in migraine headache: a review". *Cranio: The Journal of Craniomandibular Practice*. **22** (2): 132–6. doi:10.1179/crn.2004.017. PMID 15134413. S2CID 12318511

6. I. A. Nabri, "El Zahrawi (936-1013 AD), the father of operative surgery," *Annals of the Royal College of Surgeons of England*, vol. 65, no. 2, pp. 132–134, 1983.

7. M. S. Spink and G. L. Lewis, *Albucasis on Surgery and Instruments*, Wellcome Institute of the History of Medicine,London, UK, 1973.

8. I. San, H. Oguz, and H. Kafali, "Colored illustrations of pediatric otorhinolaryngologic surgical techniques of a Turkish surgeon, SerefeddinSabuncuoglu, in the 15th century," *International Journal of Pediatric Otorhinolaryngology*, vol. 69, no. 7, pp. 885–891, 2005.

9. Fleischer, Aylmer von. Moorish Europe. Aylmer von Fleischer."His work, Al-Tasrif, later translated into Latin by Gerard of Cremona, became the standard medical text for European Universities such as those at Salerno and Montpellier. This work was widely used by European medical practitioners for centuries."

10. Castiglioni, Arturo (1958). A history of medicine. A. A. Knopf. p. 274."Abulcasis (Alsaharavius or Abu'l-Qasim) (d. c. 1013) was the author of a surgical treatise which in surgery held the same authority as did the Canon of Avicenna in medicine."

11. Abū Al-Qāsim Khalaf Ibn ʾabbās Al-Zahrāwī. Albucasis on Surgery and Instruments. Berkeley: University of California Press, 1973. (676)

Ibn Sina (Avicenna) [1]

Ibn Sina (Avicenna) was a highly influential Persian polymath of the Islamic Golden Age (980–1037 AD), renowned for his vast contributions to medicine, philosophy, and science. Known in the West as **Avicenna**, he is best remembered for his monumental medical encyclopedia, **Al-Qanun fi al-Tibb (The Canon of Medicine)**, which remained a standard reference in both the Islamic world and Europe for centuries. In the field of **surgery**, Ibn Sina addressed various operative techniques, wound care, fracture management, and surgical instruments in dedicated chapters of his Canon. His work combined theoretical knowledge with clinical practice, emphasizing hygiene, anatomy, and post-operative care. Ibn Sina's methodical, evidence-based approach greatly influenced the evolution of surgery and medical education throughout the medieval world.

Avicenna's Contributions to the Art of Surgery [1, 2, 3, 4]

Avicenna was a renowned surgeon of his time. Although much of his surgical knowledge was influenced by predecessors such as Galen (AD 130–200), Rhazes, and Haly Abbas, he also introduced several original surgical techniques. [2] He viewed surgery and medicine as an integrated discipline, and to explain surgical methods, he used numerous illustrations. When performing surgeries, Avicenna followed structured principles. He treated patients in a separate surgical ward, wore green clothing during operations, and instructed his assistants to do the same. He recommended positioning the patient in a prone position after surgery in order to prevent aspiration. For wound closure, he used materials such as single strands of horsehair. [1]

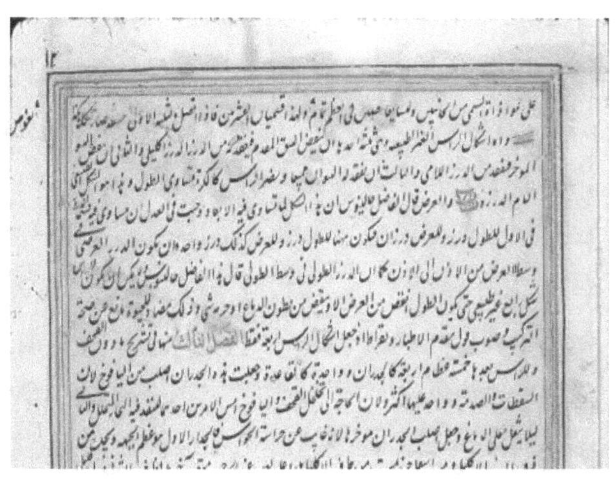

A page from Canon of Medicine showing cranial sutures by means of small diagrams (lines 2 and 4, drawn in red ink).
(Courtesy US National Library of Medicine)

Avicenna performed surgeries under general anesthesia using sterilized instruments. He proposed various compound formulations to induce anesthesia and analgesia (Canon, vol. 1, pp. 503, 511–514), including mixtures with mandragora for patients undergoing amputations, while acknowledging their toxicity and potency.

Head and Neck Surgery [1, 2]

Avicenna likely specialized in head and neck procedures [20], developing new instruments for ENT operations. He described techniques such as **tonsillectomy** and **frenotomy** for ankyloglossia (vol. 3, part 1, pp. 377–378). He appears to have been the first to describe **tracheotomy** in a choking patient:

> "... extend the head [and neck] and hold it [in that position], and hold the skin [of the anterior aspect of the neck] and incise it. It is better to hold the incised skin [in that position] using a hook. Pull the skin away until the trachea becomes visible. Incise between the two exposed middle [cartilaginous] rings .... Each two [incised] skin margins should be folded and sutured later ..."(vol. 3, part 1, pp. 374–375). [1]

He also recommended using a **hollow breathing tube**:

> "Place a hollow instrument of small diameter made of gold, silver, or a similar material into the patient's throat. This will aid breathing ..."
>
> (vol. 3, part 1, p. 371) [1]

This is considered the earliest known reference to **endotracheal intubation**.

Ophthalmology [5]

Avicenna was proficient in **ophthalmic surgery**. He described surgical treatment of **cataracts** (vol. 3, part 1, pp. 218–219) and may have introduced **eyelid surgery** techniques (vol. 3, part 1, pp. 240–251). He also provided early clinical observations on **lacrimal duct stenosis**.

Orthopedic and Neurological **Surgery** [1, 3]

Avicenna's contributions to orthopedics were substantial. He discussed bone fractures, dislocations, and soft tissue injuries in detail, and was perhaps the first to distinguish between nerves, tendons, and ligaments (vol. 1, p. 85). He also introduced suturing of nerves (vol. 4, pp. 500–512) - marking one of the earliest documented recommendations for peripheral nerve repair. He identified compartment syndrome, warning against tight bandaging that could impair circulation (vol. 4, pp. 550–552).

Abdominal Surgery [1, 6]

In describing **post-hepatic jaundice**, Avicenna linked it to biliary obstruction, citing symptoms such as pale stool, dark urine, right-sided abdominal pain, and pruritus (vol. 3, part 2, p. 327). He also discussed **bowel obstructions** (vol. 3, part 3, pp. 6–48) and designed a **squeezable enema device** (vol. 3, part 3, pp. 33–34).

Avicenna described **abdominal wall hernias** and **rectal fistulas**, including anal sphincter anatomy and treatment using silk ligatures (vol. 3, part 3, pp. 402–412) . Notably, he may have first described **postpartum vesicovaginal fistulas**:

> "… it is probable for the weight of the fetus to cause a tear in the wall of the bladder; as a result, urinary incontinence occurs and this condition remains untreatable throughout life" (vol. 3, part 3, p. 335) .

Oncology and Tumor Surgery [7]

Avicenna distinguished between benign and malignant tumors, recommending surgical excision or ligation for benign masses and wide excision for early-stage cancers:

> "If you treat a recent onset cancerous lesion, it may be possible to prevent its growth and establishment. … One should completely remove the cancerous lesion, its surrounding involved tissues and vessels …"(vol. 4, pp. 387–389).

He also appears to be the first to describe **gastric cancer**, with symptoms like chronic epigastric pain, weight loss, nausea, vomiting, and gastric wall thickening (vol. 3, part 2, p. 133).

Neurosurgery and Head Trauma [8]

Avicenna presented a structured approach to **head trauma**, using tools like trephines and elevators. He personally performed **trephination** (vol. 4, pp. 573–582) and addressed **spinal fractures**, including cervical dislocations:

"If the first vertebra of a human is dislocated, respiratory arrest may occur..." (vol. 4, p. 535).

This observation highlights his pioneering role in **neurosurgical practice**.

Urology [9, 10]

Avicenna made major contributions to **urology**, describing treatments for **urinary stones** and methods akin to **litholapaxy** and **transperineal approaches** (vol. 3, part 3, pp. 134–135, 157–160). He designed what is believed to be the **first flexible urinary catheter**:

"... the best types of urinary catheter are those made from the softest skin types. ... The tip of the catheter should be made of tin or lead; ... [the tip] should have multiple foramens, so that, when one is obstructed ... the other foramens remain open to carry the drug into [the bladder] or to pass urine ..." (vol. 3, part 3, pp. 190–191) .

Conclusion

Avicenna was a skilled surgeon who, building on the knowledge of his predecessors, made original and significant contributions to the field of surgery through his experimental approach and precise clinical observations. Much of his surgical work parallels modern practices, highlighting his advanced understanding. He stands as a key figure in the development of medieval Persian surgery and its transmission to future generations.

References:

1. Sharafkandi A (1991) The Persian translation of Al-Qanun fi al Tibb (The Canon of Medicine). Soroush Press, Tehran.

2. Kearsley G (1803) Introduction. In The Edinburgh practice of physic, surgery, and Midwifery, vol 3. Universidad Complutense, London, p xvii.

3. Afshar A (2011) A brief report about the concepts of hand disorders in the Canon of Medicine of Avicenna. J Hand Surg Am 36:1509-1514.

4. Aminrazavi M, Ibn Sina (Avicenna) (2008) In Encyclopedia of the history of science, technology, and medicine in non-western cultures. Springer, New York, pp 1119-1121.

5. Chams H (2012) Cataract surgery in ancient times. Iranian J Ophthalmol 24:1–2.

6. Ashrafian H (2013) Avicenna (980–1037) and the first description of post-hepatic jaundice secondary to biliary obstruction. Liver Int 20 November 2013, Epub ahead of print, doi: 10.1111/liv. 12350.

7. Santoro E (2005) The history of gastric cancer: legends and chronicles. Gastric Cancer 8:71–74.

8. Rahimi SY, McDonnell DE, Ahmadian A et al (2007) Medieval neurosurgery: contributions from the Middle East, Spain, and Persia. Neurosurg Focus 23:E14.

9. Madineh SM (2009) Avicenna's Canon of Medicine and modern urology: part II: bladder calculi. Urol J 6:63–68.

10. Kajbafzadeh AM (2011) Urology in Asia—Iran. Int J Urol 18:340

Ibn al-Zuhr (Avenzoar) to Surgery

https://muslimheritage.com/wp-content/uploads/2019/10/muslimheritage.com-ibn-zuhr-and-the-progress-of-surgery-ibn-zuhr-and-progress-surgery-banner.jpg

Ibn Zuhr (Avenzoar, 1093–1162 CE) was a pioneering Muslim physician, surgeon, and clinical researcher whose contributions significantly advanced the science of medicine during the Islamic Golden Age. Renowned for his precision, experimental rigor, and emphasis on practical anatomy, Ibn Zuhr laid foundational principles for modern surgery. His groundbreaking tracheotomy experiment on a goat demonstrated the safety of the procedure in humans, marking a major step in experimental medicine. A firm advocate of structured surgical training and ethical medical practice, he also emphasized preventive care, especially in managing urinary stone disease through diet. His seminal work, *Al-Taysir fi 'l-Mudawatwa'l-Tadbir*(Book of Simplification Concerning Therapeutics and Diet), remains a testament to his lasting impact on both surgical and therapeutic disciplines.

From Theory to Practice: Ibn Zuhr's Impact on Surgical Techniques

A. Detailed Contributions of Ibn Zuhr to Surgery

First Known Use of Experimental Surgery

- Ibn Zuhr was the **first to apply experimental methodology** in evaluating surgical procedures.
- His experimental approach laid the foundation for evidence-based surgical practice.
- He holds a strong claim to the title: **"Father of Experimental Surgery."**

1. Landmark Tracheotomy Experiment on a Goat[1]

To settle the controversy around tracheotomy, he **performed a tracheotomy on a goat**:

- Made an incision through the skin and trachea (windpipe).

o Maintained the wound with **regular washing using water and honey**.

o The animal **fully recovered** and lived for a long time.

o This experiment **proved the safety** and feasibility of tracheotomy in humans.

o It represented a **decisive advancement** in surgical experimentation

> "Early in my training, after reading differing opinions, I made an incision in a goat's windpipe, cutting out a small part about the size of a lupine seed. I regularly cleaned the wound with water and honey until it healed completely. The goat fully recovered and lived for a long time."[1]

Page 149 of Al-*Taysir*

2. **Challenging Ancient Surgical Dogma**

o Inherited a long-standing **controversy from Greek and Roman medicine**:

- Aretaeus (2nd century) and Caelius Aurelianus (4th century) **opposed tracheotomy**.

- Paulus of Aegina (7th century) described the procedure but it remained unpopular.

- o Even Islamic scholars like Al-Razi and Al-Zahrawi acknowledged its **risks**, though they documented favorable cases.

- o Ibn Zuhr noticed **continued reluctance** to perform tracheotomy in his time and addressed this through **experimental validation**.

    3. **Influence on Later Islamic Surgeons**

- o His successful demonstration influenced **later scholars like Al-Baghdadi and Ibn al-Quff**.

- o These physicians began to **recommend tracheotomy without reservation** in cases of airway obstruction.

- o They also described the procedure in **more detail and with refinements**, building on Ibn Zuhr's findings.

    4. **Clinical Research on Lung Ulcers Using Animal Models** [1]

- o Investigated **lung ulceration diseases** by:
    - Listening to **shepherds' observations** about diseased sheep.
    - Learning that sheep **instinctively sought specific herbs** when ill.

- o Conducted **post-mortems on sheep** to study lung pathology.

- ▪ Found **evidence of ulceration and healing**.
- This reflects an **early understanding of pathology** and the use of **natural observation** in research.

5. **Integration of Observation and Experimentation**

- Ibn Zuhr believed in the power of **clinical observation, natural behavior, and experimentation**.
- His approach reflected a **modern scientific mindset**:
  - ▪ Curious.
  - ▪ Skeptical of hearsay.
  - ▪ Committed to **direct evidence** through experimentation.

6. **Legacy in Experimental and Clinical Surgery**

- Merged **theoretical knowledge** with **practical application**.
- Advocated for a **structured, well-supervised surgical training**.
- Established **ethical and professional limits** for general physicians in surgical management.
- Left behind a rich legacy of **innovative procedures, case-based evidence**, and **disease descriptions** previously unrecorded.

B. Ibn Zuhr's Emphasis on the Importance of Practical Anatomical Knowledge for Surgeons [2]

1. Practical Anatomy for Surgical Trainees:

Ibn Zuhr highlighted the essential role of practical anatomical knowledge in surgical practice. He believed that the key to performing successful surgeries was having hands-on experience in dissection.

2. Quote on Surgical Procedure:

Ibn Zuhr advises that if a surgeon has mastered dissection, they can safely perform drainage or incision without damaging critical structures like veins, arteries, or nerves. However, if the surgeon has only theoretical knowledge of anatomy (i.e., by imitation), they should avoid performing surgeries, particularly on small, delicate organs.

Translation: "And in case you have mastered the science of dissection, then drain by the scalpel in a way that you will not come across a vein, artery, or nerve, or anything whose injury would harm the patient. But if you, like me, have not practiced dissection but only know it through imitation, stay away from the knife, as nothing you know in theory will be the same in reality, especially in the case of small organs." (Page 141 of *Al*-Taysir).

3. **Significance of Mastering Anatomy**:

According to Ibn Zuhr, mastering anatomy is a fundamental requirement for any surgeon. Only those who have practiced dissection can be trusted to perform surgical interventions safely. This emphasis on anatomy was a critical part of the medical education during the Islamic Golden Age.

Ibn Rushd, the co author with Ibn Zuhr, stated that:

"Anyone who practices anatomy will increase his faith in Allah. [3]

" من اشتغل التشريح ازداد ايمانا با لله "

C. Ibn Zuhr's Emphasis on the Red Lines in Surgical Management [1]

1. **Establishment of Boundaries for Physicians**:

Ibn Zuhr emphasized the importance of setting clear boundaries for physicians when managing surgical conditions. He believed that there were limits to what a physician should intervene with, marking a significant step in the evolution of surgery as a specialized field.

2. **The Role of the Surgeon**:

Ibn Zuhr recognized the need for specialized surgical intervention in certain cases. If a wound caused by a sharp object extends to the bones but does not penetrate deeply into the interior, he felt that the treatment could be handled conservatively with the methods he outlined.

3. **Specialist Intervention for Deeper Wounds**:

In cases where the wound does penetrate the bone, Ibn Zuhr advocated for the involvement of a specialized surgeon (referred to as "sâni' al-yad," meaning the skilled hand) to handle the situation. This distinction underscores the need for specialized expertise in certain surgical interventions.

4. **Limiting Scope of Physician's Responsibility**:

By clearly delineating when a physician should stop and refer to a specialist, Ibn Zuhr effectively set the stage for the specialization within surgery. He encouraged a shift from generalist to specialist approaches, ensuring that complex cases received the appropriate level of care.

5. **Progress in Surgical Specialization**:

This emphasis on red lines in surgical management reflects Ibn Zuhr's forward-thinking approach to the development of surgical specialties, allowing for more structured, professional, and specialized care in the medical field.

6. **Example from the Book (Management of Head Wounds)**:

Translation of Excerpt: *"If the wound caused by a sharp iron has taken into the bones and not extended to the interior, then the treatment I just mentioned is enough for you, so stick to it. However, if it did penetrate the bone, then in such a case, the surgeon (sâni' al-yad) should come and see."*

This excerpt emphasizes the importance of recognizing when a physician's intervention should stop, and when a specialist should take over.

D. Ibn Zuhr's Reliance on Clinical Observations and Contributions to Medicine [4]

1. **Emphasis on Clinical Observations**:
Ibn Zuhr relied heavily on his own clinical observations, which were central to his medical practice. He stressed the importance of firsthand experience in diagnosing and treating patients, making his approach practical and evidence-based.

2. **Skill in Differential Diagnosis**:
He demonstrated exceptional skill in differential diagnosis, carefully distinguishing between similar diseases to ensure the correct treatment. This approach highlighted his in-

depth understanding of clinical conditions and their management.

3. **Interest in Clinico-Pathological Correlations**:

Ibn Zuhr was keenly interested in clinico-pathological correlations, the connection between clinical signs and underlying pathology. His thorough investigation of these correlations contributed to more accurate diagnoses and treatment approaches.

4. **Staging and Classifying Diseases**:

Based on his clinical experience, Ibn Zuhr created a practical staging and classification system for diseases. This classification was directly relevant to their management and prognosis, allowing for more targeted and effective treatment.

5. **Innovations in Disease Description**:

Ibn Zuhr enriched surgical and medical knowledge by describing several diseases that had never been documented before. Some of the diseases he first described include:

- Pericarditis
- Mediastinitis
- Mediastinal Tumours
- Empyema
- Meningitis
- Intracranial Thrombophlebitis

- Middle Ear Inflammation
- Pharyngeal and Esophageal Paralysis
- Verrucous Malignancy of the Colon
- Fecal Fistula
- Peyronie's Disease
- Purpuric Skin Rash
- Scabies

6. **Not Just a Compiler – An Original Innovator**:
Contrary to being a mere compiler of previous medical knowledge, Ibn Zuhr was an original contributor to the field. His innovations in disease descriptions and medical classifications cement his legacy as a forward-thinking physician and surgeon.

7. **Contributions to Surgery and Medicine**:
Ibn Zuhr's detailed clinical observations, alongside his innovative approach to diagnosis and treatment, made him an important figure in the development of both surgery and medicine, significantly advancing medical knowledge during his time.

E. Ibn Zuhr's Approach to Urology and Clinical Medicine [1, 5]

1. Physician First, Surgeon by Necessity

- Ibn Zuhr was, by nature, primarily a physician.

- He was cautious about surgical interventions and preferred non-invasive treatments when possible.

- He **disapproved of surgical removal of bladder stones**, even though Al-Razi and Al-Zahrawi had made the operation safer.

2. Preference for Medical Management of Urinary Stones

- Advocated **medical remedies** to:
    - Dissolve or disintegrate urinary stones.
    - Facilitate the **spontaneous passage** of stones.

3. Early Detection and Prophylaxis

- Warned that **clear, watery urine** in a healthy individual may indicate a tendency for **stone formation**.

- Recommended **preventive measures**, including:
    - **Dietary modifications.**
    - **Herbal preparations.**

- Believed **prophylactic care** could help prevent stone formation:

  "Indeed if you managed him with this regimen I think that Allah will save him from stone formation."

4. Conservative Treatment of Acute Urinary Retention

Followed Al-Razi and Al-Zahrawi in using **conservative measures** for urinary retention due to urethral stones.

If those failed, he advocated **minimally invasive intervention** based on **endourological principles**, not open surgery.

5. Invented a New Lithotrite Tool instead of Al-Mich'ab *of Al-Zahrawi*

- Described a novel idea of a **fine probe with a diamond tip** to:
    - Reach the urethral stone.
    - **Crush it on contact**, avoiding open urethrotomy.
- This shows his **instrumental innovation** and forward-thinking in surgical technique.

6. Ingenious Use and Modification of Medical Instruments

- Modified an **ophthalmic surgical instrument** to improve its function.
- Designed **special feeding tubes** for:
    - **Orogastric feeding** (mouth to stomach).
    - **Rectal feeding** (for patients with esophageal paralysis).

- Rejected unscientific methods like **immersing patients in milk/soup** for nutrition.

7. Recognition and Legacy

- Recognized by both **Eastern and Western scholars** for his clinical excellence.

- Ibn Khaldun, Ibn Said, and George Sarton ranked him among the **greatest physicians**:

  - **"Greatest clinician in Islam after Al-Razi."**

- Gained fame in **Europe and Christendom**, with influence lasting **until the 17th century**.

Conclusion

Ibn Zuhr (Avenzoar) stands out as one of the most influential and original physicians in the history of Islamic medicine, whose legacy significantly shaped both Eastern and Western medical traditions. A pioneer of clinical observation and experimental surgery, he introduced innovative methods such as animal experimentation to validate surgical procedures, including tracheotomy. His profound emphasis on mastering anatomy through dissection, structured surgical training, and clear ethical boundaries for physician practice laid the groundwork for surgical specialization. He demonstrated exceptional skill in differential diagnosis, described diseases never recorded before him, and contributed extensively to medical knowledge with a rational, evidence-based approach. His reluctance to perform invasive procedures unless necessary and his invention of instruments like the diamond-tipped lithotrite reveal his deep commitment to patient safety and innovation. Ibn Zuhr's balanced integration of medicine, surgery, and pathology, along with his forward-thinking clinical practices, earned him enduring recognition as one of the greatest clinicians in Islamic history and a pivotal figure in the development of experimental and practical medicine worldwide.

References

1. Ibn Zuhr, *Kitab al-Taysir fi al-Mudawatwa-'l-Tadbir* li-Marwan Ibn Zuhr, Introduction, Al-Khoori M ed. Damascus: Dar al Fikr Press for the Arab Educational Scientific and Cultural Organization, 1983, 149.

2. AI-Razi M Z. *Kitab al-Hawi fi al-tibb*. Hyderabad: Osmania Oriental Publications Bureau, 1961, 154-156.

3. Ibn abiUsaybi'a. *'Uyun al-Anba' fi TabaqataI-Atiba'*. Nizar Reda, ed. Beirut: Dar Maktabat al-Hayat, 1965, 530-533

4. Dickinson EH. *The Medicine of the Ancients*. Liverpool: Holden, 1875, 37-39.

5. Ibn Sina AA. *Kitab aI-Qanun fi al-tibb*. Beirut: Dar Sadir, reprint of Cairo Boulak edition, 1877; vol. II, 507.

Ibn al-Nafīs to Surgery

علاء الدين أبو الحسن عليّ بن أبي حزم القرشي

https://en.wikipedia.org/wiki/File:Ibn_Al_Nafis_statue.jpg

Ibn al-Nafīs (1213–1288), a distinguished Arab polymath, is best known for his groundbreaking discovery of pulmonary circulation, which challenged Galenic anatomy centuries before William Harvey. An accomplished physician, anatomist, and scholar, he conducted human dissections, offering early insights into coronary and capillary circulation. Serving as chief physician at al-Naseri Hospital, his work spanned over 110 medical texts. **Ibn al-Quff, a distinguished surgeon and scholar, was among the most notable students of Ibn al-Nafis, carrying forward his teacher's legacy through significant contributions to surgery and medical literature.** Revered as "the father of circulatory physiology" and sometimes called "the second Avicenna," Ibn al-Nafīs also excelled in Islamic jurisprudence and theology, embodying the true spirit of a medieval medical and intellectual pioneer. [1]

Ibn al-Nafīs, a pioneering anatomist, conducted human dissections that led to major advances in physiology and anatomy. In addition to discovering pulmonary circulation, he offered early descriptions of coronary and capillary systems. Appointed chief physician at al-Naseri Hospital by Sultan Saladin, his medical insights earned him the title "the second Avicenna" for his remarkable contributions.[2]

Practice of dissection

Here is a concise summary of the key points regarding the debate on whether Ibn al-Nafis practiced dissection:[2]

- **Controversial Practice**: There is ongoing debate over whether Ibn al-Nafis conducted human dissections to support his discovery of pulmonary circulation.
- **Conflicting Statements**: He claimed dissection was restricted due to his beliefs, yet his writings sometimes cite dissection as a source of proof.

- **Alternate Possibilities**: Some suggest his anatomical insights may have come from surgical experience rather than formal dissection.

- **Historical Context**: Dissection was not explicitly prohibited in Islamic law or tradition, and earlier Greek medical texts encouraged it for anatomical accuracy.

- **Modern Analysis**: Scholars like Le Floch-Prigent and Delaval, through analysis of his *Commentary on the Anatomy of the Canon of Avicenna*, concluded that Ibn al-Nafis used dissection alongside clinical and physiological observations.

- **Scholarly Consensus**: Despite cultural restrictions, evidence strongly suggests that Ibn al-Nafis performed dissection to arrive at his groundbreaking conclusions.

Ibn al-Nafis: Contributions to Urology and Surgery [3, 4]

Urology (In his book "Al-Mugiza")

- Clearly differentiated between **kidney stones** and **bladder stones** by analyzing their **pathogenesis** and **clinical features**.

- Identified the distinction between **renal** and **bladder infections**.

- Classified **renal swellings** into **inflammatory** and **non-inflammatory** types.

- Advocated for **non-invasive (conservative)** management approaches to renal stones.

- Described the use of **lithontriptic (stone-dissolving)** medicaments commonly known in his time.

- Ibn al-Nafis' description of the **vesico-ureteric anti-reflux mechanism**:

  Ibn al-Nafis explained that the base and posterior part of the bladder are formed by two distinct layers. The ureters pass through the outer (superior) layer first and then continue for a short distance between the two layers before entering the bladder by penetrating the inner (inferior) layer. This structural arrangement serves an important function: when the bladder fills and expands, pressure from the inner layer compresses the ureters sandwiched between the two layers. This effectively closes off the ureters and prevents urine from flowing backward, thus maintaining one-way flow and preventing reflux.

Surgery (as described in his Kitab al-Shamil)

- Developed a **three-phase surgical framework**:
    1. **Preoperative phase** – Diagnosis and informed patient preparation.
    2. **Operative phase** – Execution of surgical procedure.
    3. **Postoperative phase** – Recovery, follow-up, and care.
- Stressed the **ethical obligations** of the surgeon towards patients and team members.
- Advocated **interdisciplinary cooperation** among surgeons, nurses, and assistants.
- Showed a deep understanding of **surgical ethics, communication**, and **medical professionalism**.

Conclusion

Ibn al-Nafis stands as a towering figure in the history of science and medicine—an innovator who courageously challenged established doctrines and illuminated the path of human anatomy with groundbreaking insights. From his pioneering discovery of pulmonary circulation to his refined understanding of urology and surgical practices, his legacy is one of intellectual courage, scientific precision, and spiritual depth. His works bridged reason and revelation, blending medicine with theology and philosophy in a way that was ahead of his time. Revered as the "second Ibn Sina" and remembered as one of the greatest physiologists of the medieval world, Ibn al-Nafis remains a symbol of the rich medical heritage of the Islamic Golden Age and a timeless inspiration to scholars across disciplines.

References:

1. Moore, Lisa Jean; Casper, Monica J. (2014). *The Body: Social and Cultural Dissections*. Routledge. p. 124. ISBN 978-1-136-77172-9.

2. Masic, I.; Dilic, M.; Solakovic, E.; Rustempasic, N.; Ridjanovic, Z. (2008). "Why historians of medicine called Ibn al-Nafis second Avicenna. *MedicinskiArhiv*. **62** (4): 244–249. PMID 19145813

3.Abdel-Halim, Rabie El-Said (12 June 2011). "Contributions of Ibn al-Nafis to the Progress of Medicine and Urology. *Muslim Heritage*.

4. Iskandar, Albert Z. *Dictionary of Scientific Biography*. pp. 602–06.

Ibn al-Quff and His Contribution to the Field of Surgery and Surgical Anaesthesia

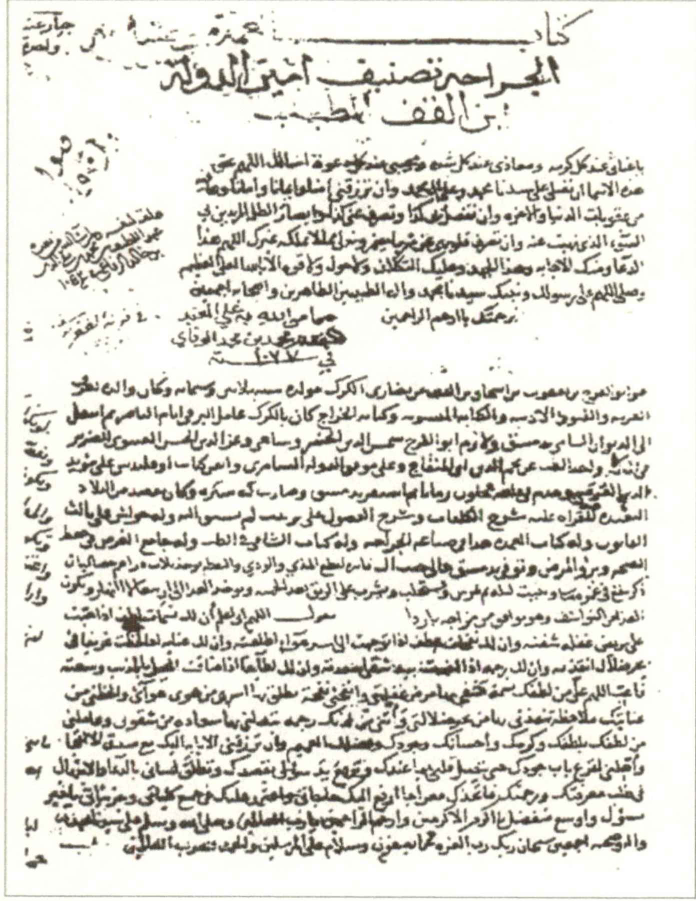

The first page of Ibn al Quff's manuscript of his surgical book al umdah with his full name and a short biography[1]

Ibn al-Quff (630 AH / 1232 CE – 685 AH / 1286 CE), a prominent physician and surgeon of the 13th century, made enduring contributions to the field of surgery, as well as to broader areas of medicine including anatomy, physiology, embryology, toxicology, and preventive medicine. [1]His surgical expertise is most thoroughly documented in his seminal work *Kitāb al-ʿUmdafīṢināʿa al-Jirāḥa* (*Basics in the Art of Surgery*), a comprehensive surgical manual comprising 20 treatises (maqālāt), with Treatises 17 and 19 focusing on traumatology and surgical disorders from head to toe.

Treatise 17, in particular, is dedicated to the discussion of wounds (*jarāḥāt*), fractures (*kasr*), and dislocations (*khalʿ*), and is divided into 39 detailed chapters. This work reflects a deep understanding of surgical pathology, classification of injuries, and appropriate interventions, both medical and surgical. It showcases Ibn al-Quff's analytical approach and his integration of earlier Greco-Arabic knowledge with original clinical insights.

Treatise (maqālā) 17 of *Kitūb al-ʿUmdafīṢināʿa al-Jirūḥa* (*Basics in the Art of Surgery*)

Chapters	Title
Chapter 1	Treatment of injury/wounds
Chapter 2	Treatment of Shock & miscarriage
Chapter 3	Treatment of fire, burn& hit injuries
Chapter 4-12	Treatment of bites of animals, insects etc
Chapter 13,14	Description of the removal & treatment of arrows & spears
Chapter 15	Treatment of skull fractures
Chapter 16	Treatment of the fracture of nasal bone& upper jaw
Chapter 17	Treatment of the fracture of lower jaw
Chapter 18	Treatment of clavicular fractures
Chapter 19	Treatment of scapular fracture
Chapter 20	Treatment of chest & rib fractures
Chapter 21-28	Treatment of the fractures of upper & lower limbs
Chapter 29	Description of dislocation
Chapter 30-35	Different treatment in the dislocation of large & small joints, vertebrae's, fingers etc

Treatise (maqālā) 19 of *Kitūb al-ʿUmdafīṢināʿa al-Jirūḥa* (*Basics in the Art of Surgery*)

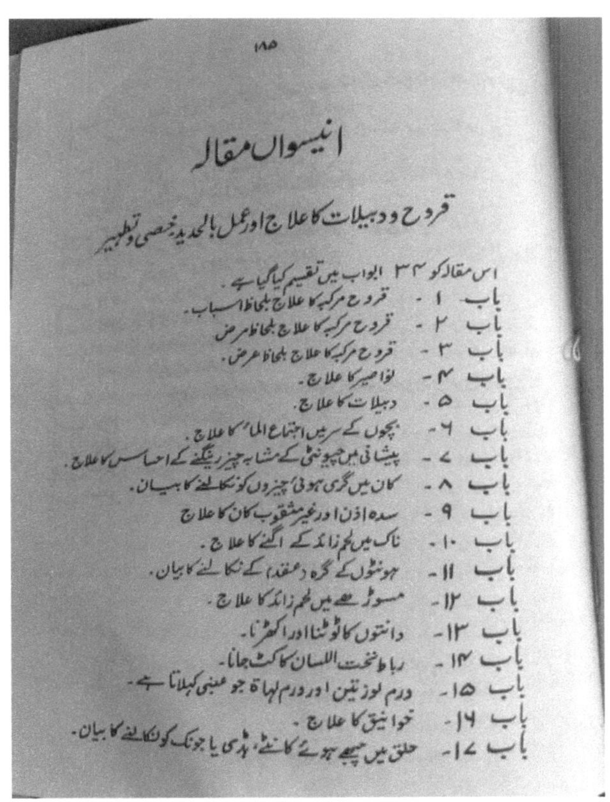

۱۸۶

باب ۱۸- مردوں میں پستان کا عورتوں کا جیسے ہو جانے اور نتوّ السرہ (ناف کا ابھرنا) کا علاج
باب ۱۹- استقاء والوں سے بذل الماء د پانی نکالنا ۔
باب ۲۰- پیدائشی طور پر قضیب اور مقعد میں سوراخ کے نہ ہونے کا علاج ۔
باب ۲۱- تطہیر و احصار کا بیان ۔
باب ۲۲- مثانہ میں احتباس بول اور زراق (پچکاری) سے حقنہ مثانہ ۔
باب ۲۳- پتھری (حصاۃ) کا نکالنا ۔
باب ۲۴- استرخائے خصیہ و استرخائے بنظر کا علاج ۔
باب ۲۵- قروح تعدد جلدہ خصیتین) کا علاج ۔
باب ۲۶- علاج خنثیٰ ۔
باب ۲۷- رتقاء کا علاج ۔
باب ۲۸- مردہ جنین کا نکالنا ۔
باب ۲۹- مشیمہ کا نکالنا ۔
باب ۳۰- بواسیر کا خزم اور قطع کرنا اور شقاق المقعد اور جریان خون کا علاج ۔
باب ۳۱- زائد اور ملتصق انگلیوں کا علاج ۔
باب ۳۲- ناخن کا کچل جانا اور زائد ناخن کا علاج ۔
باب ۳۳- علۃ البقر کا علاج ۔
باب ۳۴- ناقر نامی مرض کا علاج ۔

Among his many medical writings are: [2]

- *Al-Shāfifī al-Ṭibb* (*The Comprehensive Book of the Healing Arts*)

- *Sharḥ al-Kulliyāt min Kitāb al-Qānūn li-Ibn Sīnā* (*Commentary on the Generalities of the Canon of Medicine*)

- *Al-UṣūlfiSharḥ al-Fuṣūl* (*Rules in Commentary on the Aphorisms*)

- *Kitāb al-Jāmi ʿ al-GharaḍfīḤifẓ al-ṢiḥḥawaDafʿ al-Maraḍ* (*Compendium for Preserving Health and Repelling Disease*)

One of his most notable contributions to surgical practice is his early discussion of **surgical anaesthesia** through the use of the **soporific sponge** (*al-Esfanjah al-Murakkidah*), soaked in narcotic compounds. [3]This method of inducing unconsciousness through inhalation was rooted in the humoral theory and was innovative for his time, despite lacking the pharmacological precision of modern anaesthesia. Ibn al-Quff emphasized the appropriate selection of drugs for different routes of administration—oral, inhalational, or rectal—and warned of potential dangers and side effects.

He also demonstrated an advanced understanding of physiology by discussing the circulation of blood and suggesting the presence of **capillary connections** between arteries and veins, a concept far ahead of its time.

In sum, Ibn al-Quff represents a critical link in the evolution of surgical knowledge. His works combined theoretical rigor with practical detail, reflecting both the scientific traditions of the Islamic Golden Age and his own clinical innovations.

Ibn al-Quff's Classification and Treatment of Head Wounds (Shajja) (*Ref. 26, p.102*)

Ibn al-Quff categorizes head wounds, referred to as *shajja*, into six distinct types, each based on the depth and nature of the injury:

Types of Shajja:

1. *Ṣadiʿa* – Superficial wounds without skull fracture.
2. *Hashima* – Wounds involving fracture of the skull.
3. *Vaḍiḥa*– Wounds where the skull bone becomes visible (bone whiteness appears).
4. *Munaqqila*– Wounds in which the bone protrudes through the skin.
5. *Maʾmuma* – Wounds where the damage reaches the dura mater.
6. *Jaʾifa* – Wounds in which the injury extends into the brain ventricle.(*Ibn al-Quff, Ref. 26, p.101*)

Management of *Ṣadiʿa, Hashima, and Vaḍiḥa:*

General Measures:

- In cases of **light bleeding**, blood should be drawn from the patient to the extent tolerated.

- In cases of **heavy bleeding**, bloodletting via **cupping** is recommended.
- The patient should **avoid sour and cold** foods and beverages.
- If the patient is **weak, pure chicken broth** should be administered.
- Soft and nourishing foods such as **gruel** or **broth** are advised.
- The patient's **bowels should remain soft**; if constipation persists, an **enema** should be administered.(*Ref. 26, pp.101–102*)

Local Treatments:

1. **Shave** the hair around the wound site.
2. Apply **any of the following topical remedies**:
   - **Spiderweb** or **ebony grasshopper**
   - **Pounded sarcocolla** mixed with **egg white** and **hare's hair**
   - A **burnt and fomented dirty linen cloth**
   - **Quicklime**
   - A mixture of equal parts of the following:
     - Crushed **aloe**
     - **Myrrh**
     - **Sarcocolla**
     - **Dragon's blood**

- **Egyptian thorn juice pods**
- **Arabic gum**
- **Lemnianearth** *(Hare's hair should also be mixed into this compound.)*

3. The area **surrounding the wound** should be **anointed with rose oil**.

4. A piece of **old cotton soaked** in rose oil should be placed around the wound site.

5. During **summer**, the **wound and the head must be protected from cold exposure**.

6. **Hair over the wound** should be **left until the wound opens**, after which the wound is treated with medications used for **ulcerous wounds**.

7. **Powdered drugs** are applied on the **suture**.

8. Once the **suture is removed**, the wound should be **treated similarly to ulcerous wounds**. (*Ref. 26, p.102*) [4]

Surgical Treatment of the Last Three Types of Wounds (munaqqila, maʾmuma, and jaʾifa) (as described by Ibn al-Quff) [4]

- Ibn al-Quff discusses the treatment of **munaqqila, maʾmuma**, and **jaʾifa**—three types of deep cranial injuries described earlier in his work.

- He notes that a **skin cut may or may not be present** alongside a skull fracture.

- In cases where there is **more than one fracture**, the skin cut may also be singular or multiple.

- He emphasizes two **unique considerations in treating skull fractures**, as skull bones differ from other bones in the body:

- **Callus formation** (new bone growth):
  The skull does **not form callus internally** like long bones; only the **outer surface**regenerates bone.

- **Bandaging techniques**:
  Bandaging of skull fractures differs significantly from the treatment of fractures in other parts of the body.

Evaluation of the Cranial Wound (According to Ibn al-Quff) [4]

Shave the patient's hair to expose the wound.

- If **skin is peeled off**, cleanse the area using cotton and **examine the bone**.

- If the **broken bone is obvious to touch**, it is favorable.

- If **blood conceals the fracture**, apply **lamp oil or ink** to the wound:

- o Place **folded cloths soaked in rose oil** on the site and bandage it.
  - o After untying the bandage, **scrape and examine the bone**.
- If **black remains in the bone**, it indicates a fracture—scrape again.
- To test for a **penetrating fissure**:
  - o If ink clears off, the fissure is **non-penetrating**.
  - o If ink remains, the fissure is **penetrating**.

Check if the fissure has reached the **dura mater** and whether it is **separated** from the skull.

  - o Signs of dural separation include:
    - Presence of **pus or moisture** (CSF leakage)
    - **Pain** originating from the dura

Ibn al-Quff adds that even without these signs, **dural separation may still exist**.

Treatment of Cranial Fracture (According to Ibn al-Quff) [4]

- **Shave the patient's head completely**.
- Perform **venesection** (bloodletting).
- Administer a **cassia lincture** to **loosen the bowels**.

- Make **two intersecting incisions** at the operation site (one should include the wound).
- **Flay the skin**:
  - If **bleeding occurs**, fill the wound with **old cloth pieces**.
  - Apply **surgical pads soaked in olive oil and gallnut wine**, and bandage.
- On the **next day**:
  - Untie the bandage.
  - **Drill the bone**.
  - Ensure the patient is **seated properly** to assist removal.
  - Insert **cotton or wool in the ears** to block the sound of drilling.
- Two assistants:
  - Hold the **four corners of the skin** using soft cloth pieces.
  - **Pull skin upward** until the bone is fully exposed.
- **Bone removal techniques**:
  - For **soft skulls (e.g., in children)**: Use a **scythe or thin saw**.
  - For **thick bone**: Use a **drill** with a protrusion matching bone thickness.

- o Drill **holes spaced by the diameter of a probe**, then cut between holes.
  - o Use **tweezers, fingers, or pliers** to remove the bone.
- Place a **shell piece** between bone and dura to protect it and **remove all splinters**.
- Remaining bone fragments may **irritate the dura**, causing swelling—so:
  - o Remove all fractured bone within:
    - **7 days in summer**
    - **10 days in winter**

After Surgery: Wound Care [4]

- **Gather and place skin** over **2–3 layers of cloth soaked in rose oil**.
- Bandage and leave for **3 days**.
- Then sprinkle a **healing powder mixture** on the wound:
- Ingredients include:
  - Iris
  - Vetch flour
  - Powdered frankincense
  - Birthwort
  - Opoponax root bark
  - Myrrh

- Sarcocolla
      - Dragon's blood
  - Apply **flesh-growing medications** afterward.

Postsurgical Swelling: Causes and Treatments (Detailed) [4]

1. **Pricking Bone Fragment**
   - *Cause:* Residual bone piece pricking the dura.
   - *Treatment:* Expose and remove gently with tweezers.

2. **Tight Bandage**
   - *Cause:* Excess pressure from bandaging.
   - *Treatment:* Untie and relax the bandage.

3. **Excessive Food Intake**
   - *Cause:* Indigestion or over-nourishment post-surgery.
   - *Treatment:* Reduce the amount of food consumed.

4. **Cold Exposure**
   - *Cause:* External cold aggravating the wound site.
   - *Treatment:*

Apply **fomentation** with water boiled with:

- Marshmallow
- Fenugreek
- Linseed
- Chamomile

Mix with **rose oil** before application.

5. **Additional Measures**
   - Rub the **neck with chicken fat**.
   - Instill **heated rose oil** into the **patient's ears**.

6. **Persistent Swelling**
   - *Treatment:*
     - Bathe the patient in **hot water**.
     - Let the patient sit in the bath for sufficient time.

7. **If Swelling Still Persists**
   - *Cause:* Underlying internal imbalance.
   - *Treatment:*
     - Identify the **dominant pathogenic matter**.
     - Eliminate by:
       - **Venesection**, or

- **Laxative administration**

8. **Swelling Due to Accumulated Excreta**
    - *Cause:* Retention of bodily waste products.
    - *Treatment:*
        - Venesection or purging with **laxative medications**.

Ibn al-Quff's Contributions to Pain Relief and Surgical Anaesthesia

1 .Classification of Pain Relief [5, 6]

Ibn al-Quff, a pupil of Ibn al-Nafis, dedicated an entire chapter in *al-UmdafīṢinā'at al-Jirāḥa* to the discussion of pain relief during surgery.

He **classified pain relief into two distinct types**:

- **True pain relief** (*al-taskeen al-haqiqi*): Achieved by **eliminating the cause** of pain (e.g., healing a wound or correcting a humoral imbalance).
- **Untrue pain relief** (*al-taskeen al-ghayr haqiqi*): Refers to the use of **anesthetics** (*al-mukhaddir*) to **mask pain** without treating the underlying cause.

2. Mechanism of Action of Anesthetics (Untrue Pain Relief) [6]

Ibn al-Quff provided a four-fold explanation for how anesthetic substances relieve pain, based on the **humoral theory** and contemporary physiological understanding:

1. **Cooling effect** blocks the conduits of the spirit, preventing the transmission of pain signals.
2. **Cooling and hardening** of the vital spirit prevents its circulation and penetration into sensory pathways.
3. Anesthetics are **cold and dry** in temperament, opposing the **hot and moist** nature of pain, thereby weakening it.
4. Due to their **mildly toxic nature**, anesthetics reduce the strength of the sensory faculties, thus reducing pain perception.

⚠**Note**: Ibn al-Quff warned that this type of relief, while effective in reducing pain, could **weaken vital forces** and **trap harmful substances** in the body. He emphasized that anesthetics should be reserved for **major surgical procedures only**.

3. Anesthetic Agents Mentioned [3, 7]

Ibn al-Quff described the use of **"sleep- and insensibility-inducing substances"**, including:

- **Opium**
- **Mandrake**
- **Hyoscyamus albus (white henbane)**
- **Belladonna**
- **Cannabis sativa**
- **Cannabis indica**
- **Wild lettuce (Lactuca virosa)**

These agents were known for their **sedative, narcotic, or anticholinergic properties**, though their effectiveness via inhalation remains debated.

4. Soporific Sponge (al-Isfanjah al-Murakkidah) – Inhalational Anaesthesia [3, 7]

The **soporific sponge** was soaked in narcotic substances and applied to the nostrils of the patient to induce unconsciousness.

Though the exact **pharmacological action** remains unclear, Ibn al-Quff and others theorized that **absorption through the mucous membranes** may have played a role.

This was based on humoral and elemental theory rather than modern principles of pharmacodynamics and pharmacokinetics.

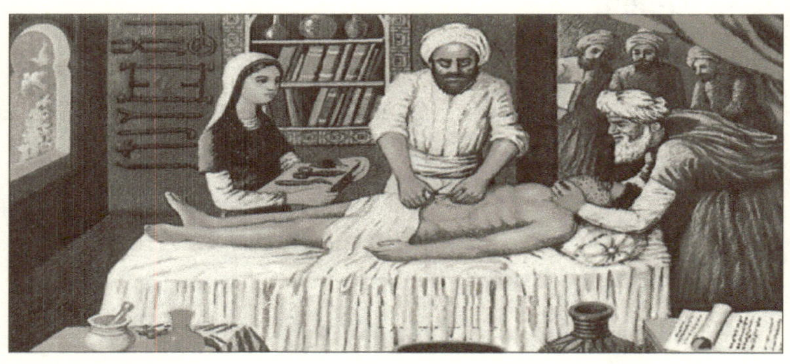

Artistic impression of Arabia anesthetic sponge, in which the surgeon operates and the tabbaee keeps the sedoanalgesic soaked anesthetic sponge over the nostril and squeezes the liquid which is absorbed by the mucous membrane of nose and mouth (published with the permission of Pan Arab anesthesia group).[3, 7]

5. Routes of Administration

Ibn al-Quff demonstrated advanced thinking by **individualizing drug administration routes**:

- **Oral (ingestion)**
- **Drinking (liquid decoctions)**
- **Inhalation** (via soporific sponge)
- **Rectal** (soaked suppositories)

He noted the **specific indications, risks, and effectiveness** of each route, reflecting a nuanced understanding of drug delivery and safety in surgical contexts.

6. Scientific and Historical Context [8]

Ibn al-Quff lived in a time of **transition from classical to empirical medicine**.His explanations of anaesthesia were grounded in **Galenic and Avicennian theories**, yet also reflected **emerging scientific insights**, such as:

- The **capillary connections** between arteries and veins.

- Awareness of **drug toxicity and systemic effects**.

- His work contributed to the **early conceptual foundation of anaesthesia**, even if not scientifically comparable to 19th-century discoveries of ether and nitrous oxide.

- In his renowned surgical treatise *The Authority on Surgery (Kitāb al-ʿUmdafīṢināʿa al-Jirāḥa)*, Ibn al-Quff dedicated a special chapter to the preparation of ethereal oils, known as *Al-Duhoun*. In this section, he described the methods of extracting and formulating approximately 34 different oils, each with specific therapeutic properties. These oils were used for various medical purposes, including pain relief, wound healing, and treatment of inflammatory conditions, reflecting his deep understanding of pharmacology and the medicinal value of botanical substances.

Conclusion:

Ibn al-Quff made significant and systematic contributions to surgical knowledge, particularly in the field of head injuries. Drawing extensively from the works of Hippocrates, Galen, and renowned Islamic scholars such as Avicenna, Albucasis, and Paul of Aegina, he offered detailed classifications and treatment strategies for cranial wounds. He categorized head injuries into six types and their treatments into medical and surgical approaches. His medical treatment involved general patient care and topical medications, consistent with earlier scholars like al-Ṭabarī, Thābit ibn Qurra, and Avicenna. His surgical guidelines—including the timing of operations and bone scraping techniques—aligned with classical sources but were also refined with his own observations, such as his explanation for the weakness of cranial callus and strategies to reinforce it.

Ibn al-Quff's understanding of cerebral anatomy, particularly the role of the ventricles in consciousness and mental function, was influenced by Hippocratic and Galenic thought. He also contextualized treatments within the humoral theory, emphasizing practices like bloodletting and purging to restore balance.

A notable innovation was his account of the **soporific sponge (Al-Esfanjah al-Murakkidah)**, an early concept of **inhalational anesthesia** using narcotic-soaked sponges. Although the effectiveness of such methods remains debated, Ibn al-Quff was among the first to discuss routes of administration, side effects, and precautions in pain management during surgery. He even anticipated elements of pulmonary circulation, showing a move beyond traditional doctrines.

Overall, Ibn al-Quff synthesized classical surgical knowledge with empirical insights and theoretical advancements, positioning himself as a pivotal figure in the evolution of medieval surgery.

References:

1. Yarmohammadi H, Dalfardi B, Kalantari Meibodi M, et al. Ibn al-Quff (1233–1286AD), genius theorist of the existence of capillaries. International Journal of Cardiology 2013; 168: e165

2.Ibn AbıUṣaybiʿa.ʿUyun al-Anbaʾfıṭabaqat al-Aṭibbaʾ. Cairo: Bulaq Edition; 2021:273-274 [in Arabic].

3. Prioreschi P. Medieval anesthesia - the spongiasomnifera. Med Hypotheses. 2003;61:213–9. doi: 10.1016/s0306-9877(03)00113-0. [DOI] [PubMed] [Google Scholar].

4. Ibnal-Quff,Amınal-DawlaYaʿqubIbnIsḥaq(c. 685/1286). Kitab al-ʿUmda fi l-Giraḥa II. In: SezginF,ed.IslamicMedicine.FrankfurtAmMain, Germany: Institute for the History of Arabic IslamicScienceat the JohannWolfgangGoethe University;1997[inArabic].page no. 98-102.

5. Feigenbaum A. Did 'ali ibn 'isa use general anaesthesia in eye operations? Br J Ophthalmol. 1960;44:684–8. doi: 10.1136/bjo.44.11.684. [DOI] [PMC free article] [PubMed] [Google Scholar]

6. Syed IB. Islamic Medicine: 1000 years ahead of its times. Online article. 1999. [accessed on 2010 Jun 15]. Available from: http://islamusa.com/im4.html

7. Keil G. Spongiasomnifera. Medieval milestones on the way to general and local anesthesia. Anaesthesist. 1989;38:643–8. [PubMed] [Google Scholar]

8. El-Gammal SY. Preparation of ethereal oils (Al-Duhoun) by Ibn Al-Quff (13th century A.D.). Bull Indian Inst Hist Med Hyderabad. 1996;26(1-2):59-64. PMID: 11619397.

Introduction of Surgery in India: A Historical Perspective

The advancement of surgical knowledge in India, particularly during the Islamic Golden Age and the Mughal era, reflects a unique blend of traditional Indian medicine and the influence of Greco-Arabic science. The Mughal period, especially under Emperor Shah Jahan (d. 1658), is often regarded as a zenith for the healing arts in India.

Surgical Flourishing under Shah Jahan [1]

During Shah Jahan's reign, medicine and surgery received royal patronage and significant scholarly attention. Shah Jahan himself was considered not only a capable ruler but also a man of scientific interest. One of the most notable figures of this era was **Hakim Nur al-Din Abdullah**, also known as *Masih al-Zaman*, a surgeon of great repute. In 1645, he authored a comprehensive medical treatise titled **Tibb-e-Dara-Shikohi**, named after **Crown Prince Dara Shikoh**, Shah Jahan's son and a great patron of the sciences.

This treatise discussed several surgical techniques, including:

- **Bathing therapy**

- **Vein section (phlebotomy)**
- **Cupping**
- **Cauterization**
- **Use of leeches for therapeutic purposes**

The manuscript is notable for including **illustrated anatomical portraits**, clearly depicting body parts, a rare and valuable tool for medical teaching in its time. Dara Shikoh, although tragically killed by his brother Aurangzeb, was a visionary interested in the sciences. His extensive personal library included numerous works on medicine, signifying his intellectual influence on the era's medical developments.

Influential Medieval Scholars and Their Surgical Insights [2, 3]

Beyond the Mughal court, other significant figures contributed to the foundations of surgical science in the Islamic world and India:

Abd al-Latif al-Baghdadi (d. 1231) was a scholar and physician who conducted what is considered one of the earliest documented **postmortem autopsies** during the famine in Egypt (c. 1200 AD). He examined over 2,000 skulls and correctly deduced that the **mandible is a single**

bone, contradicting Galen's long-standing belief that it was composed of two bones. He also identified the **sacrum** as being made up of **five fused bones**, another departure from Galenic teachings. His observations, though groundbreaking, were overlooked for centuries due to their publication in a geographical text and prevailing reverence for ancient authorities.

Ibn al-Quff (d. 1286), in his Kitāb al-'Umda fi 'l-Jirāḥa (The Basics in the Art of Surgery), provided detailed discourse on **anatomy, drug therapy, wound management, and tumors**. Notably, he hypothesized the **existence of capillaries**, describing the connection between arteries and veins through minute, invisible pores—centuries before William Harvey's confirmation of blood circulation. His two-volume work was published in Hyderabad, India, in 1937, and reflects a sophisticated understanding of physiology and surgical care.

Mansur bin Muhammad of Shiraz, in 1396, compiled the **Kitab al-Tashrih (Book of Anatomy)**, renowned for its **colored anatomical diagrams**. These illustrations attracted the attention of modern historians like Dr. Karl Sudhoff, who suggested that they might trace back to ancient Alexandrian anatomical traditions. This manuscript represents a valuable confluence of Islamic and earlier medical knowledge.

Imad al-Din Mahmud Shirazi, in 1565, authored **Sharh Tashrih al-Qanun**, a detailed commentary on the anatomical sections of Avicenna's *Canon of Medicine*. A two-volume manuscript of this work survives in the Raza Library in Rampur, India, dated to 1576.

Daud al-Antaki, a later physician, composed a noteworthy treatise titled **Risala fi al-Tashrih al-Uzam (Treatise on the Anatomy of Bones)**, further expanding the corpus of anatomical and surgical literature available to scholars and practitioners.

Contributions and Legacy

The works of these physicians illustrate a period when **anatomy and surgery were deeply studied** through dissection, empirical observation, and experimentation—often in defiance of prevailing dogma. Their efforts not only enriched the Indian and Islamic medical heritage but also **preserved and enhanced Greco-Roman medical traditions**, passing them through centuries into the modern era.

India, particularly during the Mughal period, became a vibrant center for medical learning where **surgical knowledge was not just preserved but actively expanded**, blending indigenous, Persian, and Arab influences. The richly illustrated treatises and practical techniques described above are a testament to the **scientific spirit and clinical sophistication** of medieval Indian medicine.

References:

1. PoonamBala, Medicine and medical policies in India, NY 2007, page 52.
2. Quoted in - PlinioPrioreschi, History of Medicine Byzantine and Islamic Medicine, USA, 2001, page 301.
3. E.G. Browne, Islamic Medicine, Goodword Books, Nizamudin Market, New Delhi, 1921, reprint 2003, page 93.

Hippocratic Oath

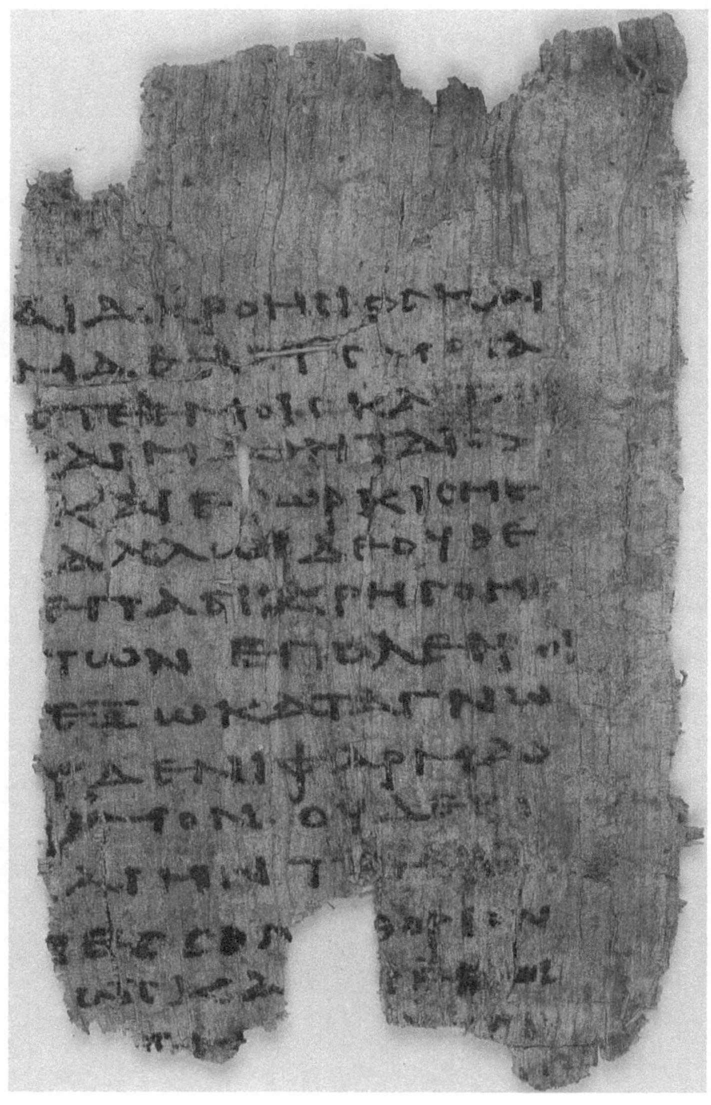

A fragment of the oath on the 3rd-century <u>Papyrus Oxyrhynchus</u> 2547.[1]

The original oath was written in <u>Ancient Greek</u>, between the fifth and third centuries BCE.[1] Although it is traditionally attributed to the Greek doctor <u>Hippocrates</u> and it is usually included in the <u>Hippocratic Corpus</u>. The oldest manuscript containing the oath dates to roughly the 10th–11th century, held in the <u>Vatican Library</u>, although [2] papyrus fragments of the oath have been found as early as the 3rd century AD.

Below is the Hippocratic Oath, in Ancient Greek, from the 1923 Loeb edition, followed by the English translation:[3]

ὄμνυμι Ἀπόλλωνα ἰητρὸν καὶ Ἀσκληπιὸν καὶ Ὑγείαν καὶ Πανάκειαν καὶ θεοὺς πάντας τε καὶ πάσας, ἵστορας ποιεύμενος, ἐπιτελέα ποιήσειν κατὰδύναμιν καὶ κρίσινἐμὴνὅρκοντόνδε καὶ συγγραφὴν τήνδε: ἡγήσεσθαι μὲντὸνδιδάξαντά μετὴντέχνην ταύτηνἴσα γενέτῃσινἐμοῖς, καὶ βίουκοινώσεσθαι, καὶ χρεῶνχρηΐζοντιμετάδοσιν ποιήσεσθαι, καὶ γένοςτὸἐξ αὐτοῦἀδελφοῖςἴσον ἐπικρινεῖνἄρρεσι, καὶ διδάξειντὴντέχνην ταύτην, ἢνχρηΐζωσι μανθάνειν, ἄνευμισθοῦ καὶ συγγραφῆς, παραγγελίηςτε καὶ ἀκροήσιος καὶ τῆςλοίπης ἁπάσης μαθήσιοςμετάδοσιν ποιήσεσθαι υἱοῖςτεἐμοῖς καὶ τοῖςτοῦἐμὲδιδάξαντος,

καὶ   μαθητῇσισυγγεγραμμένοις   τε   καὶ
ὡρκισμένοιςνόμῳἰητρικῷ, ἄλλῳδὲοὐδενί. διαιτήμασί
τεχρήσομαι ἐπ᾽ ὠφελείῃ καμνόντων κατὰδύναμιν καὶ
κρίσινέμήν,   ἐπὶ   δηλήσειδὲ   καὶ   ἀδικίῃεἴρξειν.
οὐδώσωδὲοὐδὲφάρμακον οὐδενὶ αἰτηθεὶς θανάσιμον,
οὐδὲὑφηγήσομαι   συμβουλίην   τοιήνδε:
ὁμοίωςδὲοὐδὲγυναικὶ πεσσὸνφθόριονδώσω. ἀγνῶςδὲ
καὶ ὁσίωςδιατηρήσω βίοντὸνἐμὸν καὶ τέχνηντὴνἐμήν.
οὐτεμέωδὲοὐδὲμὴνλιθιῶντας,
ἐκχωρήσωδὲἐργάτῃσινἀνδράσι   πρήξιοςτῆσδε.
ἐςοἰκίας δὲὁκόσας ἂνἐσίω, ἐσελεύσομαι ἐπ᾽ ὠφελείῃ
καμνόντων,   ἐκτὸςἐὼν   πάσηςἀδικίηςἑκουσίης   καὶ
φθορίης,   τῆςτεἄλλης   καὶ   ἀφροδισίωνἔργων   ἐπί
τεγυναικείων σωμάτων καὶ ἀνδρῴων, ἐλευθέρωντε καὶ
δούλων. ἃ δ᾽ ἂνἐνθεραπείῃ ἴδω ἢ ἀκούσω, ἢ καὶ
ἄνευθεραπείης   κατὰ   βίονἀνθρώπων,   ἃ   μὴχρή
ποτεἐκλαλεῖσθαι   ἔξω,   σιγήσομαι,   ἄρρητα
ἡγεύμενοςεῖναι   τὰτοιαῦτα.   ὅρκονμὲνοὖνμοιτόνδε
ἐπιτελέα ποιέοντι, καὶ μὴσυγχέοντι, εἴη ἐπαύρασθαι
καὶ βίου καὶ τέχνηςδοξαζομένῳ παρὰ πᾶσινἀνθρώποις
ἐςτὸν αἰεὶχρόνον: παραβαίνοντιδὲ καὶ ἐπιορκέοντι,
τἀναντία τούτων.

*I swear by Apollo Healer, by Asclepius, by Hygieia,
by Panacea, and by all the gods and goddesses,*

making them my witnesses, that I will carry out, according to my ability and judgment, this oath and this indenture. To hold my teacher in this art equal to my own parents; to make him partner in my livelihood; when he is in need of money to share mine with him; to consider his family as my own brothers, and to teach them this art, if they want to learn it, without fee or indenture; to impart precept, oral instruction, and all other instruction to my own sons, the sons of my teacher, and to indentured pupils who have taken the Healer's oath, but to nobody else. I will use those dietary regimens which will benefit my patients according to my greatest ability and judgment, and I will do no harm or injustice to them. Neither will I administer a poison to anybody when asked to do so, nor will I suggest such a course. Similarly I will not give to a woman a pessary to cause abortion. But I will keep pure and holy both my life and my art. I will not use the knife, not even, verily, on sufferers from stone, but I will give place to such as are craftsmen therein. Into whatsoever houses I enter, I will enter to help the sick, and I will abstain from all intentional wrong-doing and harm, especially from abusing the bodies of man or woman, bond or free. And whatsoever I shall see or hear in the course of my profession, as well as outside my profession in my intercourse with men, if it be what should not be published abroad, I will never divulge, holding such things to be holy secrets. Now if I carry out this oath, and break it not, may I gain for ever reputation among all men for my life and for my art; but if I break it and forswear myself, may the opposite befall me. — Translation by W.H.S. Jones.

Modified Version:

This version is still in use today by many US medical schools:[4]

> I swear to fulfill, to the best of my ability and judgment, this covenant:

> I will respect the hard-won scientific gains of those physicians in whose steps I walk, and gladly share such knowledge as is mine with those who are to follow.

> I will apply, for the benefit of the sick, all measures [that] are required, avoiding those twin traps of overtreatment and <u>therapeutic nihilism</u>.

> I will remember that there is art to medicine as well as science, and that warmth, sympathy, and understanding may outweigh the surgeon's knife or the chemist's drug.

> I will not be ashamed to say "I know not", nor will I fail to call in my colleagues when the skills of another are needed for a patient's recovery.

> I will respect the privacy of my patients, for their problems are not disclosed to me that the world may know. Most especially must I tread with care in matters of life and death. If it is given me to save a life, all thanks. But it may also be within my power to take a life; this awesome responsibility must be faced with great humbleness and awareness of my own frailty. Above all, I must not play at God.

> I will remember that I do not treat a fever chart, a cancerous growth, but a sick human being, whose illness may affect the person's family and economic stability. My responsibility includes these related problems, if I am to care adequately for the sick.

> I will prevent disease whenever I can, for prevention is preferable to cure.

> I will remember that I remain a member of society, with special obligations to all my fellow human beings, those sound of mind and body as well as the infirm.

> If I do not violate this oath, may I enjoy life and art, respected while I live and remembered with affection thereafter. May I always act so as to preserve the finest traditions of my calling and may I long experience the joy of healing those who seek my help.

References:

1. *Edelstein, Ludwig (1943). The Hippocratic Oath: Text, Translation and Interpretation. Johns Hopkins Press. p. 56. ISBN 978-0-8018-0184-6.*

2. *"Codices urbinatesgraeciBibliothecaeVaticanae: Folio 64(Urb.gr.64)". Vatican Library: DigiVatLib. 900–1100. p. folio:116 microfilm: 121.*

3. Hippocrates of Cos (1923). "The Oath". *Loeb Classical Library.* **147**: 298–

299. doi:10.4159/DLCL.hippocrates_cos-oath.1923.
Retrieved 6 October 2015.

4. "The Hippocratic Oath. *PBS*. 27 March 2001.

<u>Endnotes</u>

1. **The Edwin Smith Papyrus** (c. 1600 BCE), one of the oldest known medical texts, presents a case-based surgical manual emphasizing anatomical observation, wound treatment, and rational diagnostics—likely reflecting the teachings of Imhotep.

2. **Sushruta**, revered as the "Father of Surgery," authored the *Sushruta Samhita*, a landmark surgical compendium. It describes over 300 operations and 120 surgical tools, advocating dissection, suturing, hygiene, and postoperative care centuries ahead of its time.

3. The concept of **KhayootiJarahiya**—ligatures and suturing—is extensively detailed in Unani and Ayurvedic traditions. Sushruta pioneered the use of natural threads, ant heads, and bark fibers for wound closure, showcasing remarkable biomedical ingenuity.

4. The **pedicle graft**, introduced in *Sushruta Samhita*, is an early example of plastic surgery. This technique, especially in nasal reconstruction, laid

foundational principles for modern reconstructive surgery.

5. **Al-Razi (Rhazes)**, the 9th-century Persian polymath, championed clinical observation in his monumental *al-Hawi*. His writings covered abscess drainage, bone setting, and wound cauterization—fusing empirical science with surgical dexterity.

6. **Al-Zahrawi (Albucasis)**, in his magnum opus *Kitab al-Tasrif*, illustrated more than 200 surgical instruments. From forceps to lithotomy knives, his tools were designed with precision and ergonomic awareness, some closely resembling modern instruments.

7. Among his many innovations, Al-Zahrawi was the first to document **ligation of blood vessels to control hemorrhage**, and he developed refined approaches in **neurosurgery**, **dental surgery**, and **gynecology**—centuries before European advancements.

8. **Ibn Sina (Avicenna)** integrated Greco-Arabic medical theory in *The Canon of Medicine*, covering surgical treatment of tumors, fractures, abdominal pathology, and head trauma. Though primarily a

physician-philosopher, his surgical influence was profound.

9. **Ibn Zuhr (Avenzoar)** revolutionized surgical methodology by insisting on **practical anatomical dissection** and **clinical testing** over theoretical reliance. His work brought clarity to urological procedures and safe surgical boundaries.

10. **Ibn al-Quff**, in *Kitab al-'Umda fi 'l-Jirāḥa*, provided one of the most systematic classifications of **head wounds (shajjah)**. His descriptions laid groundwork for modern cranial surgery and injury management.

11. His detailed account of the **soporific sponge (al-isfanjah al-murakkidah)**—a blend of opium, mandrake, and henbane for inhalational anesthesia—illustrates the early conceptualization of pharmacologically induced unconsciousness.

12. The **Mughal surgical renaissance**, particularly during Shah Jahan's reign, gave rise to richly illustrated treatises like *Tibb-e-Dara-Shikohi*, which fused Greco-Arabic and Indian surgical philosophies, contributing to a vibrant medical ecosystem.

13. **Imad al-Din Mahmud Shirazi**, a Safavid scholar, refined surgical practices through empirical methods. His integration of Galenic theory with anatomical observation advanced the precision of medieval surgery.

14. The **Hippocratic Oath**, though Greek in origin, was adapted across Islamic and Indo-Persian traditions. Its core tenets—compassion, ethical restraint, and a duty to heal—resonate through generations of healers and are echoed in this text.

15. Surgical instruments across ancient civilizations—crafted from bronze, steel, ivory, and obsidian—reflect a keen understanding of **ergonomics, metallurgy, and clinical purpose**. Each tool was a synthesis of craft and care.

16. The **cross-cultural transmission of surgical knowledge**, through translation movements in Baghdad, Córdoba, and Delhi, created a confluence of Egyptian, Indian, Greco-Roman, and Islamic science—shaping the surgical heritage this book celebrates.

The First Surgeons: The Evolution of Operative Skill and Instrumentation in Early Medicine *is a richly woven tapestry of surgical history that traces the evolution of operative care across ancient civilizations. From the anatomical rigor of the Edwin Smith Papyrus and the surgical brilliance of Sushruta to the empirical precision of Al-Zahrawi and Ibn Sina, the book highlights the global mosaic of early medical ingenuity. It explores pioneering techniques such as pedicle grafts, ligatures, and anesthetic sponges, while showcasing the remarkable diversity and craftsmanship of surgical tools fashioned from bronze, steel, ivory, and more. Central to its narrative is the cross-cultural transmission of knowledge—how translations and intellectual exchanges across Egypt, India, the Islamic world, and Europe forged a shared legacy of healing. By spotlighting forgotten innovators and the ethical codes that guided them, First Surgeons celebrates the enduring spirit of surgical inquiry and the operative techniques & instrumentations that shaped its earliest chapters.*

Index